rethink.
the way you live

Amanda Talbot

Photography : Mikkel Vang

CHRONICLE BOOKS
SAN FRANCISCO

This book is dedicated to my family and,
in particular, my husband, Oliver Heath, who has been
my support, my rock, and my love. He has held my hand
continuously with an enormous heart in the rough
storms and the sunshine.

RETHINK

VERB
TO THINK AGAIN, REFLECT,
OR REVIEW OR ALTER
ONE'S IDEAS

TO CONSIDER AGAIN WITH
A VIEW TO A CHANGE OF
DECISION OR ACTION

NOUN
A REVIEW OR APPRAISAL
OF ONE'S PREVIOUS THINKING,
A REASSESSMENT

A DRASTIC AND
FAR-REACHING CHANGE
IN WAYS OF THINKING
AND BEHAVING

SYNONYM—RECONSIDER

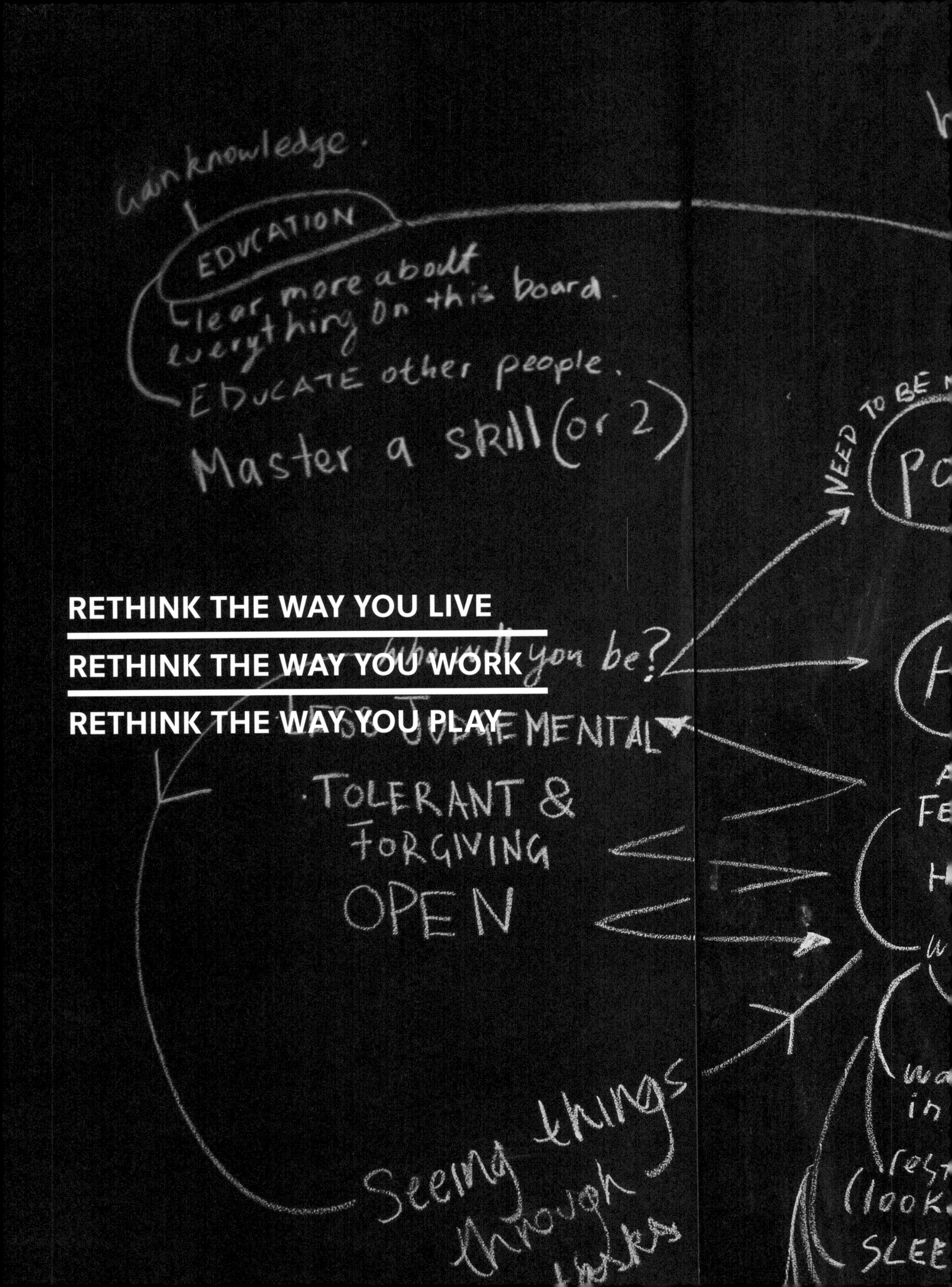

Gain knowledge.

EDUCATION

Lear more about everything on this board.

EDUCATE other people.

Master a skill (or 2)

NEED TO BE

PO

who will you be?

LESS JUDGMENTAL

• TOLERANT & FORGIVING

OPEN

RETHINK THE WAY YOU LIVE

RETHINK THE WAY YOU WORK

RETHINK THE WAY YOU PLAY

Seeing things through

SLEE

more energy.

EAT RIGHT → HEALTH

TRANSCENDENTAL MEDITATION

grow your own food.

POSITIVE

IVE

UTOPIA

PINESS

AL
GS

NESS.

ives this?

COMPASSION

plants move
ght breeze.
nd relaxing
r myself)

ACTIONS

(ULTURE.

CONTENTS

"Helplessness
and being unsure
about the future
are creating anxiety
and panic in a
concerned population
who feel there is a
sense of urgency
to make a change in
the way they live."

Amanda Talbot

rethink emerging trends

In 2009, my life changed. I left my high-profile editorial position at British *ELLE Decoration* magazine with no plan as to what I would do next. Why? I had fallen out of love with "shelter" magazines. I could no longer connect with the content of these types of magazines because they didn't relate to the way I lived. My friends and most of my colleagues were increasingly removed from the reality of these magazines, too. I didn't know anyone who had a glossy home filled with expensive designer furniture. My home was filled with IKEA, Habitat, flea market finds, press gifts, and handmade bits and bobs.

Another factor also came into play: moving the personal story into a much bigger picture. The global economy crashed, friends lost their jobs, and I was feeling scared and overloaded.

Just like fashion, times have changed when it comes to designing our homes. "Design is not for philosophy, it's for life," says Issey Miyake. We used to think we had to have high-end design furniture in our homes to be desirable, but now it's about having creative flair. We don't need a home found in magazines, but what we do need is a living environment that fits perfectly to our families' lifestyles.

**THE BIG FIVE
THAT HAVE ROCKED
OUR WORLD**

**1. ENVIRONMENT
2. ECONOMY
3. TECHNOLOGY
4. TERRORISM
5. CHINA**

**THESE FACTORS
CREATE A
SENSE OF FEAR,
DISTRUST, AND
AN OVERRIDING
FEELING THAT
THERE IS A LACK
OF CONTROL OVER
THE BIGGER
GLOBAL PICTURE.**

I began spending hours online reading blogs and looking at Flickr, discovering how people of all ages and from all corners of the world were living inside their homes, the places they called home. And what I saw was that "home" was very different from the conventional ideas we have of what a home is. I became fascinated with how strangers used their beds and bedrooms, how people sat in a chair, how teenagers were photographing their personal spaces. Inadvertently, I started documenting living trends that were happening across the globe.

As a result, my whole attitude and approach to design was turned upside down. I began questioning the conventions that had been in place for so long. I was looking at rooms in homes in a completely new way and found myself asking questions: Do we need an office in a home when there is only a laptop and iPad in sight? Is a bedroom only used for sleeping? Can a kitchen become an edible farm? Matching living trends with good design is no longer just about color, function, and aesthetics. It is about creating a product, an idea, a space that can enhance our life and help us deal with what obstacles this changing world is throwing at us. How do we create a home that will bring out the best in us?

We need to be surrounded by great design that will feed and nurture us. If we are aware of our needs and desires, we can make the right choices. It's not just about the individual, it is also about considering the global community.

Let me be clear from the outset. I am not an academic. My research is purely done from my observations, personal experience, and curiosity about life and humankind.

Rethink will take you on a tour of the globe, visiting lifestyle mavericks who can show us how we can rethink the way we live and improve our life.

Rethink isn't a pretty book. It is a book that hopefully is a strong catalyst to change how you think about your current lifestyle. *Rethink* is about making you aware of your lifestyle and the trends that are rapidly unfolding around the world. By absorbing the trends that work for you and your lifestyle, you will be able to create a space that will fit you and your life like a glove.

Rethink is not a bible for living. I am not going to preach to you about style, taste, and designers. I'm not going to come over all warm and reassuring and say "home is where the heart is." *Rethink* is not that kind of book.

This is about real-life trends that are happening now and will affect us all, changing priorities about how we live in our personal spaces.

We've lived through the "greed is good" '80s, the recession of the '90s, the decadence of the noughties, and are now facing the Global Financial Crisis (GFC), climate change, and the change of traditional political and social structures throughout the world.

Put simply, we are responding to our environment and renovating our caves for safety and security. A change in the stability of the world on a global scale is having an enormous impact on how we live, and in response, the human race is learning to adapt and evolving to survive in the current climate.

Our world as we've known it has changed, but it's not all bad news. As we retreat into the safety of our homes, our caves, people all over the world are pushing aside the gloom and doom and looking at ways to build a better world from the grassroots up.

Environment

Being bombarded with constant information about global climate change from unprecedented heat waves, flash floods, melting snow caps, rising sea levels, diminishing rain forests, erosion, biodiversity loss, water shortages, and escalating disease, is it any wonder so many of us are scared about the future of our planet and the impact it will have on our lives?

Economy

With people across the developed world losing jobs and houses, unable to pay bank loans or household bills, it means millions of individuals are facing a bad credit rating. In a capitalist society, this has significant repercussions. The question is, how do people live in a world based on a financial credit rating system when their current credit rating has been destroyed?

Our basic quality of life is dictated to most of us by our access to credit. In many first-world countries, bad credit means that you are unable to get a loan for a house or car, rent a home, or even have a phone contract. With no way out of this downward spiral, many people affected by the collapse of traditional economies are reaching a breaking point, forced into what feels like hopeless situations. Poverty in America hit a record of 49 million in 2010, which equals 16 percent of the population. Millions of Americans have received foreclosure notices, and tens of billions in real estate assets have been written off as losses by banks.

Bewilderment has turned into anger as the economic crisis impacts the lives of families through rising unemployment, reduced wages, and collapsing asset values.

Almost one in four people in the European Union (EU) was threatened with poverty or social deprivation in 2010. A staggering 115 million people, or 23 percent of the EU population, were designated as poor or socially deprived. The main causes are unemployment, old age, and low wages, with more than 8 percent of all employees in Europe now classified as the working poor.

The European Debt Crisis is dramatically affecting the economic and political landscape across Europe. Greece's (370 billion euro debt) and Italy's (1.9 trillion euro debt) broken economies have caused pandemonium across Europe and the world. Protests and violence broke out in Italy and Greece as governments in both countries had put in place unpopular austerity measures and economic reforms demanded by the EU.

This new and unstable world is taking the lives of families across the globe into uncertainty. With the environment and economy being under such great threat, it is making many individuals rethink and consider their beliefs, values, and responsibilities. Families are hurting financially, and their security in their home, health, and quality of life is hanging by a thread. So many are reaching a breaking point and feeling hopeless about their future.

In 2008, economies around the world collapsed, our planet was announced to be in dire crisis both economically and environmentally, war and terror went hand in hand with fear, and technology advanced quicker than saying "Apple." Respect and trust in our government was and is at an all-time low, and we discovered our supermarkets are not telling the truth about where our food comes from. Feels a little like "the end is nigh," doesn't it?

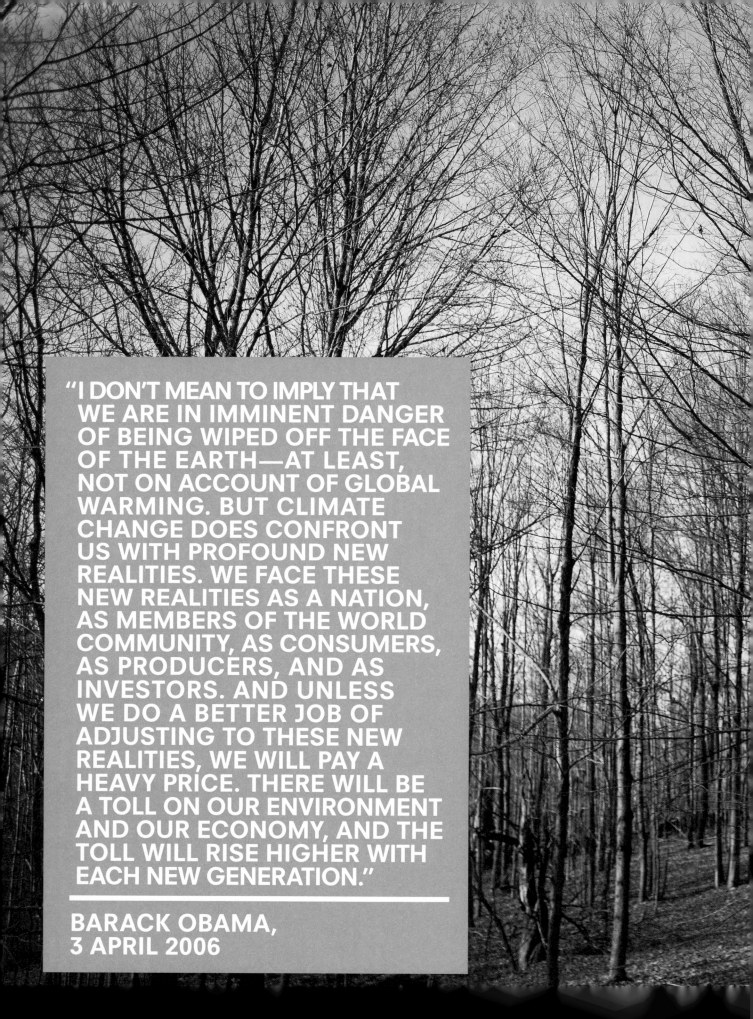

"I DON'T MEAN TO IMPLY THAT WE ARE IN IMMINENT DANGER OF BEING WIPED OFF THE FACE OF THE EARTH—AT LEAST, NOT ON ACCOUNT OF GLOBAL WARMING. BUT CLIMATE CHANGE DOES CONFRONT US WITH PROFOUND NEW REALITIES. WE FACE THESE NEW REALITIES AS A NATION, AS MEMBERS OF THE WORLD COMMUNITY, AS CONSUMERS, AS PRODUCERS, AND AS INVESTORS. AND UNLESS WE DO A BETTER JOB OF ADJUSTING TO THESE NEW REALITIES, WE WILL PAY A HEAVY PRICE. THERE WILL BE A TOLL ON OUR ENVIRONMENT AND OUR ECONOMY, AND THE TOLL WILL RISE HIGHER WITH EACH NEW GENERATION."

BARACK OBAMA,
3 APRIL 2006

As the euro continues to drop, hardworking individuals across Europe are nervously watching their savings becoming devalued and the cost of credit rising.

Emerging markets, such as Central and Eastern Europe and Asia, could also be hit by the eurozone crisis. The International Monetary Fund (IMF) said, "While these markets have been quite resilient to shocks and developments in major economies in the past year, recent indicators have weakened significantly and the general business climate has deteriorated."

Technology

Technology is evolving within the blink of an eye and humans are being forced to adapt to the overload of information to keep up with trends. Intuitive, instant, social, access to information on a huge scale is just one of the miraculous effects of the rise of the geek. Computer firms, including Apple and Microsoft, are researching the technology that will turn spaces and inanimate objects such as bedrooms, offices, pencils, even cans of soft drink into active participants in our lives. These objects will soon be equipped with small devices that can communicate with each other and the world at large. Soon our fridge will be able to detect how much food is inside and then communicate directly to the supermarket and organize a delivery at a time when it knows you will be home. With all of the positive contributions of technology there are also pitfalls in our wired-up world. Privacy is already a problem but a fully-wired world integrating outside organizations with your personal life will challenge the concept of what friends, governments, and companies should know about us. Someone will have access to your eating patterns, your political interests, and other personal details, clearing the way for a marketing bombardment. The sheer wall of technology that is facing us means that we might become desensitized as to what is going on or older generations will be terrified of being left behind on the technology superhighway.

Terrorism

Terrorism has impacted lives since September 11, 2001, when the world saw two hijacked planes flown into the twin towers in New York City. The attacks shattered Americans' sense of security, threw the nation into a state of emergency, and triggered a years-long war in Afghanistan and an extended worldwide "war on terrorism." Former American president George W. Bush described the attacks as an "act of war."

Technology is evolving the way we live. Our homes are no longer the sanctuary where we disconnect from the world. They're now the hub where we have become ever more connected. We now shop, socialize, keep tabs on our kids, and work all in one spot. The speed at which technology is being integrated into our lives is often so complex it is sometimes incomprehensible, but it's clear we need to reconsider the design of our homes.

Suddenly, in the sheltered Western world, there was a real fear about death and instability. Our lives changed overnight. The rise of this unknown fear introduced us to a new and different definition of evil. We saw trusted politicians become as manipulative, terrifying, and distrustful as the dictators we were told our lives were threatened by.

East vs. West

Stability and security are two ideals we work toward daily. Vulnerability and fear are two states we work hard to avoid in our lives. China's extraordinary economic growth is turning it into a superpower. Europe's debt crisis, the United States' political paralysis, and Japan and China promoting direct trading of the yen and the yuan without using the dollar signals a shift in power. China's economic dominance is bringing into question the diminishing strength and state of Western economies.

China seems like a threatening monolithic juggernaut, but at the moment we are only guessing at what China might do as a superpower. But is it all bad? Firstly, the new wealth for China's 1.3 billion people means more global consumers. Secondly, the global economy is no longer solely dependent on the United States.

Brands are pushing into China to find a lucrative marketplace to survive.

There is a large group of people who don't see China in a positive role. An economically powerful China seems to be causing fear and a sense of vulnerability within many of us, despite countries such as Australia attributing its survival of the global crisis in 2008 to their boom in exports to China.

Countries such as Australia are nervous that they are too dependent on China for their growth and what may be helping them financially may hurt their country politically and strategically. Racism could be playing a part in this fear, but I believe it is much deeper and more complex than this. It is not just economics; it is now ideological.

Europeans and Americans have dominated the world for many centuries, so it is understandable that they are uncomfortable that another country is taking their place. China's economy is modeled on "state capitalism" and their policies seem to give little consideration to other nations. They seem to be grabbing whatever natural resources they can from across the globe, and their beliefs in democracy, human rights, and civil liberties aren't aligned with those espoused by the West.

"The way we feel about our life and all it involves dictates our behavior. Our perception about the world changing affects our emotions and these emotions affect our behavior. Changes in perception is the way forward to change differently and more intuitively."

Edward de Bono

Friction between major global economic powers is increasing as trade relationships are becoming unstable. "Made in Britain" and "Buy American" are now marketed strongly in the press, and government policy throughout the United Kingdom and America is geared to make their local manufacturing and economy stronger against China. Both countries have developed initiatives and legislative acts to compel individuals and the US Congress to buy only goods and services made in their countries. The US House of Representatives passed the China Currency Manipulation Bill, legislation that would punish China for undervaluing its currency and harming the competitiveness of US manufacturers and exporters. This move has heightened trade tensions between the two countries.

We are facing one of the biggest global changes since the United States took over global leadership from the British Empire. With the uncertainty about what it all means for the direction of global civilization with the rise of the East, many people feel uneasy. Generally people don't like change and uncertainty. Perhaps this is why we are so fearful of China.

Fight or flight—the modern solution

When times are tough, our behavior and choices revert back to our caveman ancestors. Early man faced a lot of dangers from his environment, making living very stressful. As a result, the fight-or-flight response evolved to help him evade or battle those dangers to help him survive.

The fight-or-flight response, coined by Harvard University physiologist Walter Cannon in 1915, is something that influences how we live and work today. Contemporary life is fast-paced, busy, filled with activity and external stresses. But it doesn't have to be like this. Many people are taking flight, leaving their high-powered jobs to follow their dreams and aspirations or to stand up for issues that they are passionate about. People are trying to get back some control in their lives. Call it the modern-day "fight-or-flight" response.

We are all trying to find some way to gain a sense of control by searching out pleasure, joy, fulfillment, happiness, and love— all states that help us enjoy life. When those feelings are overcome by anger, stress, fear, hunger, depression, and the breakdown of families and relationships, we look to reclaim our memory of how the good life can feel. This is survival. Survival is the choice of fight or flight to inject positivity back into your life. Behaviors and values that satisfied our needs in the past may not satisfy us in different circumstances. This causes a rethink of values and ideals to create and live a fulfilled life. There is a global crusade of individuals and families discovering a new and better lifestyle improved by learning from mistakes in this last decade.

In our urban environment we increasingly feel how difficult it is to find time to spend with family and friends. What's more, we feel inadequate when we can't afford the lifestyle promoted in mainstream media. People are now reclaiming their lives by being innovative and re-creating different lifestyles that suit the individual rather than following the herd.

Humans are tough and adaptable. We are survivors. We may feel as if we have lost control over the last few years, but we are fighting or flighting from our current situation to get it back. Breaking away from what had been the social norm, individuals are discovering what used to satisfy them may not be the case anymore. They are redefining a new and better lifestyle that will give them happiness and fulfillment.

SURVIVAL

NOUN
THE ACT OR FACT
OF SURVIVING

Talking about a revolution

There has been an incredible backlash against governments, unemployment, and poverty across the planet as demonstrated by the Arab Spring to the youth riots in London and Occupy Wall Street. The revolution is about a new way of thinking. The unprecedented circumstances and events that we are experiencing are sparking the big meaning-of-life questions:

Who am I?
Why am I here?
What's the point of living?
What's life about?
Am I happy in my work, the place I live, and my relationships?
What do I want to get out of life?
What do I really love to do?
Would I rather have quality of life with my family over financial happiness?

There is also a revolution going on in our homes. New values are reflected in how we use our personal living spaces. This revolutionary personal journey is getting us to look at things from a new angle and approach things differently. New ideas and possibilities are waiting to be explored and adopted into our lives. As a result, our homes are not simply the product of economic forces but instead represent optimism, too; our desire to elevate everyday existence to a more poetic plane.

We can fulfill people's needs and desires only when we understand what they are. We need to dig deep and understand their priorities, values, inspirations, likes, and dislikes.

REVOLUTION

NOUN
A DRASTIC AND
FAR-REACHING CHANGE
IN WAYS OF THINKING
AND BEHAVING

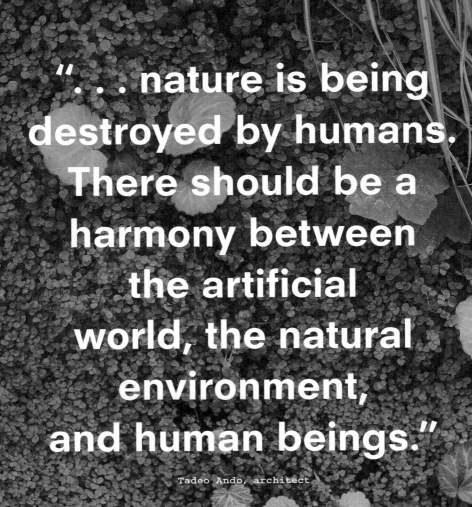

"... nature is being destroyed by humans. There should be a harmony between the artificial world, the natural environment, and human beings."

Tadeo Ando, architect

rethink

living with

nature

As a result of overworked urbanites fighting to regain some "slow time" and reconnect with nature, a green revolution is sweeping through our homes. The more we are away from nature, the more we feel the need to be connected with it.

Over 50 percent of the world's population is living in cities and towns, and most don't have large residential outdoor spaces. Overcrowded urban living is making land an expensive commodity. Small terraces and balconies are a common urban compromise that allows city dwellers to have access to their own outdoor space. Increasingly, many of us desire to live in peaceful and self-sufficient surroundings away from a world that seems unstable and precarious. According to the Future Foundation, 45 percent of twenty-five- to forty-four-year-olds feel the need to be closer to the countryside.

Innovative people, such as well-known botanist Patrick Blanc, are bringing the rain forest to urban concrete-jungle walls. For thirty years or more, Blanc has been the creator of rural elements for city views with his indoor and outdoor vertical gardens. Two of his impressive works can be found at Musée du Quai Branly in Paris and on the Athenaeum Hotel in London, featuring over 12,000 plants.

27

Nature is good for us. It's good for our physical and psychological well-being. If we lose our interaction with nature by living in such urbanized spaces, what could the outcome be?

We are like caged animals in a zoo removed from our intrinsic relationship to nature. Instinctively we know there is far more to existence than the urban lives we are living. A farmer who works on the land understands the seasons, knows when the land is fertile and when it needs to be nurtured. The big question is how we are going to stay in touch with nature when it is being built out by concrete and roads and rapidly replaced by urban sprawl.

Nature in our urban landscape and homes is critical for connecting half of the world's people with the natural environment. The experience and contact the majority of the world has with nature is more likely to occur in the city or home rather than a rural setting. The more urban our lifestyle, the bigger the need for a connection with nature. It's not just about bringing the country into the city. It is not about our immediate well-being. We need to look after nature if we want nature to look after us.

For centuries, the Japanese have been a great influence on how we can incorporate nature into our homes by incorporating natural fibers and materials and blurring the boundaries between indoors and out. The Japanese emphasis on connecting with nature comes from the roots of the Shinto religion. Shinto temples incorporated the belief that Kami (Shinto gods or deities) live inside of every living thing, from the mountains to water to rocks and trees. To be closer to Kami the Shinto temples were built around trees, rocks, and mountains in harmony with nature.

A rooftop conservatory in Ekoda, Tokyo, has been transformed into a spectacular bathroom. Japanese firm Suppose Design Office successfully incorporated nature into the bathing sanctuary by using clusters of large potted plants.

There's a need for more people-friendly conservation that allows wildlife to coexist with human development. A London house by Bere Architects covered in a green roof has varying soil depths for native ecological habitats including a wildflower meadow and a thriving colony of bees.

"We are seeking familiar forms to bring comfort, solid materials to give weight. Robust and heavy textiles to reassure." Ilse Crawford, designer

Delicate design isn't cutting it for most of us. We are harking back to primitive aesthetics celebrating the imperfections of natural materials, highlighting our current yearning for simplicity and honesty.

LONDON Landscape gardening is no longer restricted to the outdoors. With an increasing amount of homes across the globe being built on small plots in unsightly urban areas, it's not surprising there is a growing desire to have vibrant landscaped gardens indoors. Succulents are a fantastic choice to bring the green inside for those who don't have a green thumb. These hardy houseplants are perfect for those who are busy and travel a lot for work. There are so many different varieties in different sizes and colors. Display them as a group rather than scattered around the house. Not only do they add more impact, this way it is easier to remember to water them all at the same time.

NEW YORK People in the United States spend an average of 65 percent of their time at home and as much as 90 percent of their time indoors, according to a national survey conducted by the American Lung Association in May 1999, so it's important to have plants indoors.

ANTWERP Indoor air pollution caused by harmful chemicals and other materials can be up to ten times worse than outdoor air pollution. Designers are using plants to help purify the air by filtering air that has been contaminated by mass-produced goods. Designer Julio Radesca de Carvalho discovered that twelve houseplants per person would be enough to filter air in one room indoors.

INTERNATIONAL TREND
rethink: greenery

*from home
with love x*

A vista of trees or a water view helps people harness the wild and ever-changing environment. Studies
have shown that when we look out a window and see a natural vista, our stress levels drop instantly.

Paula Leen—Poetryworld, Akkrum, Friesland

Bringing the
natural world inside

"Our home is not perfect but we love that. We want it to be natural and filled with textures. It's wild and raw."

Living with nature can be achieved in different ways. One of the best ways to connect with Mother Earth is to fill your home with natural materials. I visited an incredible home situated in a village called Akkrum owned by Dutch felt artist Paula Leen from Poetryworld. She has designed her home harmoniously with the opposing forces of the countryside. The soothing space is filled with raw timbers, soft lamb's wool, masculine earthy tones, and fragile fauna.

Paula shares her home with husband, Kees, who runs a boating business, and their daughters, Lotte and Silke. The building is an old converted barn with an artisanal feel. Paula and Kees have self-built the inside of the home. "I surround myself with things that have a soul and tell a story. We love to make things with our hands. We make our own furniture with our hands because it is a part of us. We are not architects but you can feel our heart and soul inside because we have made everything," says Paula.

The couple used lots of iron and old wood—materials that tell a story. "I seek inspiration everywhere in nature, music, art, history, and fashion," says Paula. "The kitchen island I designed was built by a local metalworker and the cupboards were made from the original wooden floorboards and antique doors." Paula used a lot of dark gray for her color scheme inspired by the clay soil surrounding the house and the local landscape. "Gray is perfect for a gentle and subtle background. It helps provides a restful atmosphere," says Paula.

"When something is perfect I get bored
very quickly but imperfection I continue to love."

Paula Leen, Poetryworld, Akkrum

From the moment we have lived in this house (1989), situated in Akkrum village in the Dutch province of Friesland, nature has been an important element in our house. My house has a calming effect on people.

With so many busy influences in the world it is important our home has the feeling of a calm stillness and a quiet you expect when lying on a grass patch in a secluded forest while gazing at a blue sky watching the clouds rolling by.

It's like an island, our own universe, a place where we are not under pressure, but where we can relax.

I have a dream . . .

I feel that there is too much stuff in our capitalist world, I dream of a world where everybody has enough.

According to me there is enough for everyone, if we divide it fair.

I hope that we all start to take care and responsibility for our Earth.

I long for self-reliance, for creativity, for uniqueness, for self-expression, I yearn for goods exchanged at recycle shops, growing your own vegetables, I would like to live together with respect for nature, enjoy her beauty, feel gratitude for food and all the beauty she gives us . . . and for being alive.

Paula Leen

Along with the pared-back colors, she has used tactile textures, mixing distressed woods with cozy wool. Natural daylight is a key feature to this calming interior. Paula has opted to forgo curtains in the open-plan living and kitchen area. This allows the light that changes constantly during the day to stream indoors through a long narrow window in the living room and the skylights in the kitchens. There isn't a corner that hasn't been curated with Paula's eye. She seeks inspiration everywhere; in nature, music, art, history, and fashion.

Paula uses her home as a backdrop for her beautiful felt and wool accessories she makes on the ground floor in her workshop. Rugs, throws, and lampshades are a few of the beautiful objects she makes with her hands and are found in boutiques across America and Europe. The raw, wild, and natural fibers mirror the beautiful home she has created. "Nothingness is everything to me. I love natural objects that don't have meaning. Finding a place for them in my home is my power and this gives my house power," says Paula.

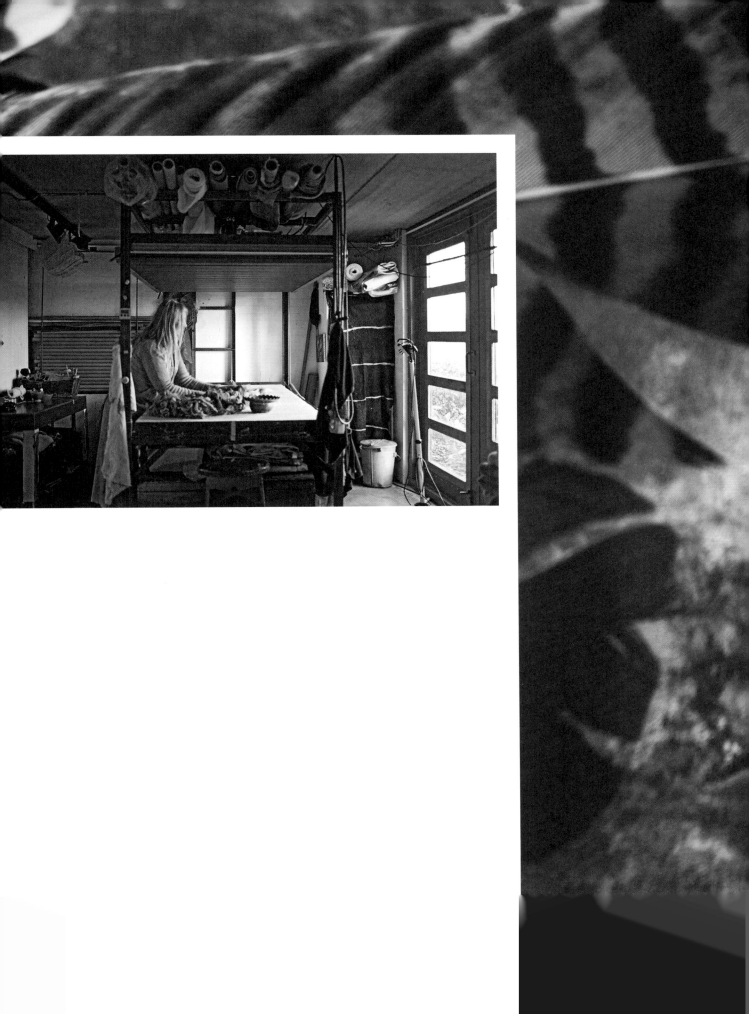

OWNERS: LEE FELDMAN + YUKIKO TANIGUCHI
LOCATION: GREEN WALL, AMSTERDAM

Architects are reexploring how to incorporate the abandoned backyard into urban homes that are sited on narrow plots of land surrounded by neighboring houses. The indoor gardens are treated as extra rooms inside the home, literally bringing outside elements indoors. Lush green plants, flowerbeds, textured stones, and wood provide a living, vibrant, and beautiful interior to add new dimensions.

One of the most exciting and modern examples I have seen so far across the globe in bringing a garden indoors is the home of Lee and Yukiko, designed by Dutch architects i29. I visited when the outdoor temperature was in the minuses but inside it was like visiting a home in tropical Australia. The stark white minimalist open-plan space contrasts with a crisp, lush,

green interior vertical wall covered in plants. "We don't live in a big space but we wanted to be able to connect with the outdoors. Integration of nature is an important aspect for us. I'm from Canada and Yukiko is from Japan. Nature plays an important role in traditional Japanese culture and I have been surrounded by vast natural spaces growing up," says Lee.

With the couple's busy lifestyle it was important the garden was low maintenance and evergreen. Green Fortune, who installed the vertical wall, are like an updated version of a hired gardener. They maintain the wall once a month, trimming and replacing plants.

It's when you walk to the back of the house to the bedroom and bathroom that are tucked inside a wood-clad box that you get the strong impact of

Vertical gardens make it possible to have lots of greenery without losing floor space. Besides being impressively beautiful the plants also provide oxygen and humidity to improve air quality.

Living with Nature:
Lee Feldman + Yukiko Taniguchi
_ Reconnecting with nature in the city
_ Bringing gardens indoors
_ Including vertical gardens
_ Using natural fibers and materials
  including cotton, leather, linens,
  wool, wood, stone, and water

Landscape gardening is no longer
With more homes across the globe
there is a growing desire to have

the green wall. "It's so peaceful and life feels stress free—waking up in the mornings and looking onto the wall," says Lee.

I have been to homes that have tried to bring nature inside and the results have not been as romantic as the idea. I once went into a home with a waterfall and flowing water throughout. The reality was the space was swarming with mosquitoes. Another home I visited had trees and grass indoors but they were all dead when I visited. Another home had a lush vertical garden but it was overbearing and didn't feel like the plants belonged inside the space. What I love about this planted wall is there is a sheet of glass in front which gives the feeling of the garden belonging outside even though it is inside. The glass gives a sense of protection, security from the outdoors. It's like sitting in your bed on a rainy night knowing you are tucked away safely. The feeling completely changes when you go behind the glass wall and walk up the staircase that leads to a roof garden. Suddenly you feel adventurous and mischievous and there is a strong sense of freedom.

restricted to the outdoors.
being built on small urban plots
landscaped gardens indoors.

COPENHAGEN Storage doesn't have to be ugly. Soren Korsggard architects have made use of an overbearing roof iron support frame by stacking chopped firewood that's needed throughout a Danish winter. The contrast of the manmade iron with the natural wood makes a space that could have been cold into a raw beauty.

RECLAIMED WOOD

AMSTERDAM Add rustic charm to your home with weathered and tactile wood. Using plenty of timber for your walls and floors mixed with moody cool colors creates a strong sense of a beautiful European forest inside your home.

NEW YORK Rugged wood has been used to reinforce the owners' connection to the rural landscape outside. Using worn wood reflects the need to live with honest, sustainable materials and creates a space filled with texture and earthy tones. **AKKRUM** In this kitchen, discarded old timber doors have been reimagined to provide just the right finish for kitchen cabinets. Mixing timber with natural linen curtains helps keep the open kitchen clear of clutter.

LONDON Give recycled wooden floorboards a new lease on life by using them as cladding on your interior walls. Create a cozy cabin-like bathroom by utilizing the wood on all walls. Soften the space with feminine, vintage floral textiles. You will have a treasure if you find and reuse an old bathroom sink and taps.

"My philosophy is best summed up by the phrase 'plain, simple, and useful.' Such things may not win many design prizes, but neither do they go out of fashion."

Sir Terence Conran, grandfather of British design

rethink

back

to basics

Simplicity isn't about being a cold, hard minimalist. A different way of looking at simplicity is to take note of the Japanese aesthetic of *wabi sabi*. It is difficult to translate it directly into a Western sensibility but it is a way of finding beauty in imperfection and profundity in nature.

Wabi sabi is a way of being that champions the simple, slow, and uncluttered and reveres the natural cycle of things along with authenticity above all else. Applied to the home, *wabi sabi* insinuates a warm minimalism that celebrates the human effect rather than the machine-made or mass-produced object.

Wabi sabi encompasses objects that resonate with the maker's touch, things with soul. It is an intuitive mind-set rather than a stylized decorating "look."

Sometimes less is more. A pared-back approach to decorating can fill a home with elegance and charm. To help reduce anxiety caused by the recession, a nostalgic yearning for all things past and comforting is becoming more prominent.

We don't want just stuff anymore. A purchase has to make sense— to our bank balance and for the planet. Less is increasingly more. In our mass-produced world where everything feels and looks the same, interior design is responding by keeping elements of design basic within the home. Outside of the home we are increasingly looking for the simple things in life; in our fashion, packaging, restaurants, cooking, shopping, homes, and gardens. We are sourcing quality, economical products with no brand attachments. We have become more discerning and question why we should buy certain things.

Designs masked with gizmos and gadgets make us question quality. Why has a designer added gimmicks to their design? What are they hiding? If you are confused about how your home should look and feel, use the iconic Duralex glass for inspiration and ask how and if it can be improved.

Form and function

Good design adds value. There is a new readiness to swap the glossy and aggressively marketed for ordinary, everyday household items; thoughtfully designed objects for everyday. Clean lines, no direct brand attachment, well-made and timeless products are great basics to kit out your home. I like to think of them as sturdy, unpretentious friends who will always be there for you. This can be a feather duster, enamel dishes, a wooden chopping board, and, of course, a classic Brown Betty teapot.

One of my favorite shops in London is Labour and Wait. They showcase a range of ordinary and everyday household items. Presenting them as timeless marvels of both form and functionality. I feel so calm and relaxed when I visit. I'm not bombarded with brand choice. I'm embraced with familiarity. It's perfect. It reflects my philosophy: simplicity matters in this modern and complicated world.

We are preferring handmade, nostalgic, simple, and honest designs in our home over a brand name. We want to respect the long tradition of the object from use to manufacturing but we do sometimes want a contemporary feel. We want our home to boast 21st-century modern conveniences but we want our technology to be smart, integrated, and seamless.

Another consideration with going back to basics is the awareness of the environmental impact that all the discarded mass-produced domestic debris is having on the planet. This awareness creates the need to make buying decisions based on sustainability—can the object be reused and kept for a lifetime? Taking this approach and buying with thoughtful awareness reflects the beliefs in integrity and authenticity. A leaning toward craftsmanship and the handmade object is also a result of this conscious decision making, too. As we edit our lifestyles we seek out products and interiors that evoke an emotional response—products and interiors that offer us comfort and reassurance.

Responsible purchasing is about sourcing quality, economical and nostalgic products with no brand attachment. We don't want overcomplicated design. Simple is best.

"Simplicity is the ultimate sophistication."

Leonardo da Vinci

Simplicity is the key to the back-to-basics movement and color plays an integral part in achieving this. Bold is out and cool, restful, subtle, calming, chalky hues are the preferred choice. Back to basics embodies the luxurious simplicity of space. Smooth chalk finishes in the softest gray tones are balanced with gentle whites, greens, and charcoal. Wheat gives a gentle golden glow of warmth. Untreated wood provides rich, natural warmth, balanced with cooling granite and slate. Neutral colors give you a beautiful canvas to decorate with. Limited use of color and pattern creates a sophisticated environment to reboot in.

I HAVE IDENTIFIED A SIMPLE
BACK-TO-BASICS CHECKLIST:

CONSIDER WHAT YOU BUY

DON'T FALL INTO FASHION FADS

ASK YOURSELF, WILL I BE
BORED WITH THIS OBJECT BY
NEXT YEAR?

WILL IT ENDURE MY FAMILY'S
LIFESTYLE?

DO I REALLY NEED ANOTHER ONE?

We are recognizing our world is changing and everything we know will be different in the years to come. We just don't know what the outcome is going to be. It's hard to feel stable while there is so much change. The idea now is to create solidity with the objects that surround us. Over time industrialization and globalization have produced emotionless design but we are seeing a shift toward conscious consumerism. Materials, manufacturing processes, and ethics are all being examined. We want to surround ourselves with objects that will hold some form of nostalgia that will not date or need replacing. The DNA for these austere times is calm, considered, intelligent, not showy design.

"A DURALEX DRINKING GLASS
EMBODIES THE ORDINARY
DONE EXTRAORDINARILY WELL.
DESIGN FOR ME IS NOT ABOUT
CRASS NEOPHILIA, NOISY
SHOW-BOATING, OR ANNOYING,
MERETRICIOUS STUFF THAT
SCREAMS FOR ATTENTION.
I ALSO THINK ECONOMY IS
THE MOST TESTING OF ALL
DISCIPLINES. SO A DURALEX
DRINKING GLASS MEETS MOST
OF MY CRITERIA: USEFUL,
AFFORDABLE, INDESTRUCTIBLE,
AND IT ALSO WORKS IN ALL
SIZES. NOT, I CONCEDE, A THING
OF GREAT BEAUTY, BUT ONE
OF REAL EVOCATIVE POWER.
A SLUG OF SUPERMARKET RED
IN A DURALEX GLASS AND YOU
ARE IMMEDIATELY TRANSPORTED
FROM WAITROSE TO PUGET-
THÉNIERS. SIMPLE OBJECTS THAT
TELL STORIES ARE WHAT I ENJOY;
DURALEX IS VERNACULAR CHIC,
THE VERY BEST OF FRANCE.
LIKE ALL QUALITY DESIGN,
IRRESPECTIVE OF PRICE IT HAS
LASTING VALUE."

STEPHEN BAYLEY,
CURATOR, CRITIC, CONSULTANT,
AND COMMENTATOR

Finding beauty in
the everyday

"Sometimes it is better to dream about something than to actually have it."

Katrine Hansen and her partner have been urban nomads for most of their adult life but two years ago they wanted to put down their roots back in their hometown. Their home is a simple black barn-shaped building. Raw wood floorboards and white walls follow this line of simplicity. "I love the light in our home; it helps the space feel very calm. We call it our base and we come here to get some peace and quiet, time away from the hustle," says Katrine. The home isn't a minimal space but it contains only what is necessary to their lifestyle. As Katrine outlines, "I can't breathe in clutter. I need space around me." Daily rituals when they are home are important to them both. "Our simplest but most important ritual at home is our coffee in the morning. We prepare it in two ways. My boyfriend prefers an espresso and I prefer the pour-over cowboy-style coffee," Katrine tells me.

Katrine's approach to life is about not getting caught up in the day-to-day, focusing on the little things that make a day special. This approach is reflected in her home. "It is comforting having the sense of being close to the water. I can take my swims throughout the year and walk to the jetty in a robe without anyone raising an eyebrow because they're most likely in a robe as well," Katrine says.

Katrine Hansen—Copenhagen, Denmark

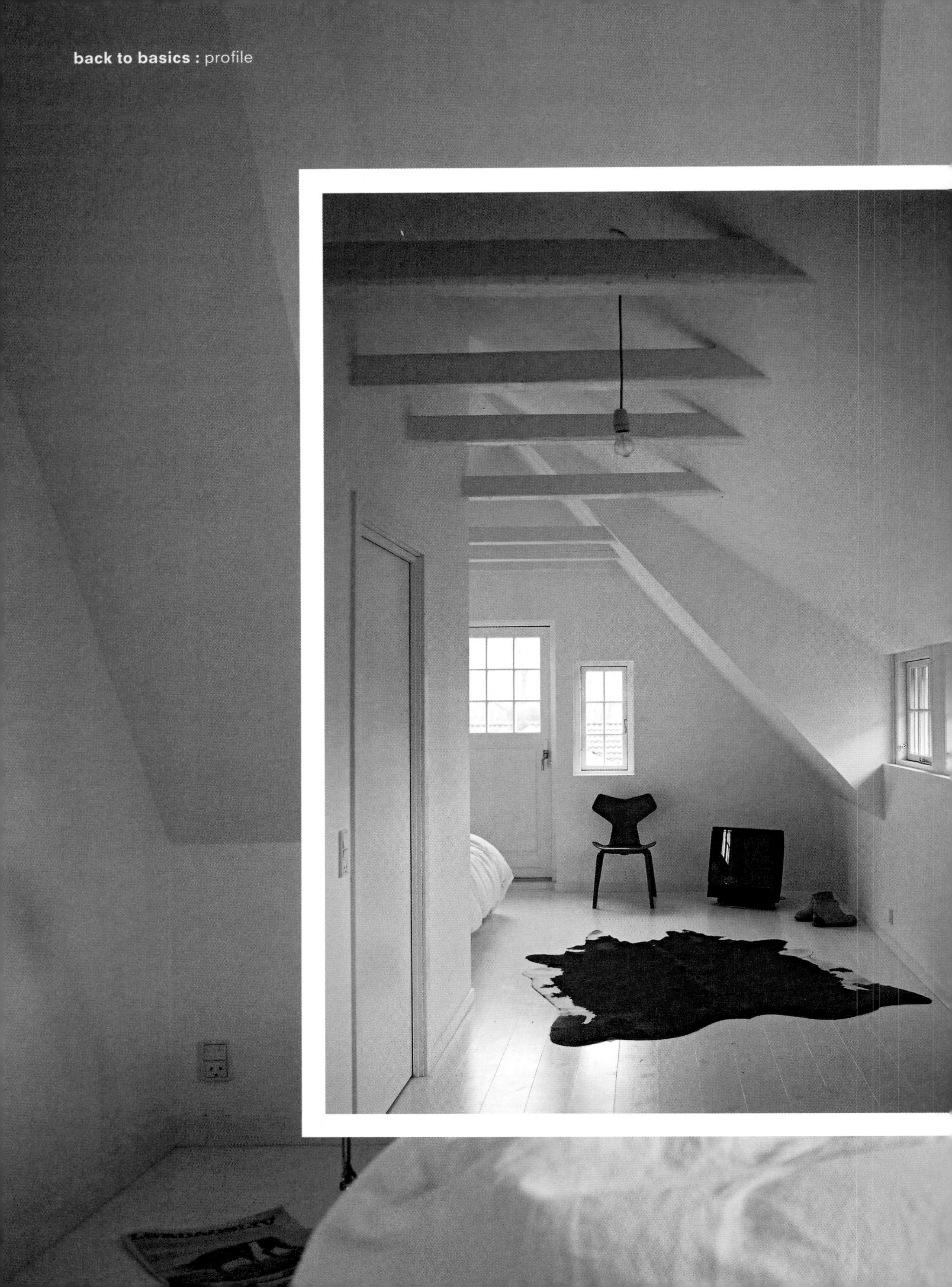

These days there is more emphasis on people decorating their homes with a mind to having objects that will be handed down to family members. The idea of "heirlooms" is making a comeback. When we make a decision to acquire something for our homes it is a more conscious decision looking at, for example, why we need a particular chair and how we are going to use it. Included in this decision is the object's "longevity" and how it will last for our children and our children's children.

"Our furniture is a mix of new and old. We either have beautiful, well-made, handcrafted objects that mean something to us or they just simply fix a problem. If something does the job, it's very likely it will stay. The dining table is from my grandmother. It used to be the kitchen table at my grandparents' farm. It's a little bit unsteady and bruised. When it's moved it has to be disassembled, and now the legs are harder and harder to fix. But it has this amazingly clever way of extending, it fits twelve people, and really does the job," Katrine explains. "In contrast, steel shelving units in the kitchen are mass-produced, super cheap, and bought in a split second. We were unpacking our shipping boxes, realizing we didn't have enough cupboard space. I love them for being unpretentious and they do their job so well."

Products with a sense of history and the ability to transport you to a place you would like to be are becoming more and more important. It's not so much the vintage find but the nostalgic feel. The homeowners I met who are paying homage to basic elements that surround us share a passion for beautiful, well-made, handcrafted objects chosen from the heart, whether utilitarian or decorative. "The cow hide in my bedroom reminds me of Australia, and the colorful painting in my dining room by former graffiti artist Rus Kitchen transports me back to the laneways in Melbourne. The pendant lights in the kitchen were bought in Gertrude Street, Melbourne, and it is exactly the same as the one we had in our small studio flat in St. Kilda. The deck chair reminds me of my first flat in Copenhagen. During this time in my studio flat I only had the deck chair, a bed, and my grandmother's table," Katrine says.

"To help us survive this world we have made it a place to breathe and have a break. The way we designed our home changes our mood when we walk inside and helps us get through the day to day. I feel more at peace when I'm home. I can recharge, rethink, and prepare. My dream is more about how I would like to see the world move forward, as we all need to breathe and reconsider once in a while."

OWNERS: RICHARD PETERS + HEIDI DOKULIL
LOCATION: SYDNEY, AUSTRALIA

Architects, designers, and home-owners are becoming more humble when it comes to residential design. It's as if many of the middle class have discovered aspiration isn't about having a home that is large, showy, and full of bling and are instead focusing on the private, unpretentious, and sustainable. Richard Peters and Heidi Dokulil have challenged the concept "bigger is better," and have created an unassuming home that is full of spirit and soul.

Richard Peters tells his story. "Our house may not seem fancy but our aim was to turn a back-lane shed into a home. While we now have a contemporary home we haven't lost the character or the spirit of the original shed. Our home is straight-forward, uncomplicated, plain, and simple. This is the life we aspire

to in this complicated and fast-paced world.

"Tucked away at the end of a lane in the Sydney suburb of Randwick is our 797-square-foot/74-square-meter simple brick industrial home built in 1890 by two Irish blacksmiths (brothers) to house their coach-building business. Over the past 120 years the building has also operated as a motorcycle repair shop, a secondhand washing machine warehouse, a builder's workshop, and more recently a studio for local artists. Having grown up in the area, I knew the building well and when it came up for sale in 2003, Heidi and I took a leap of faith and invested in it.

"While so much now happens inside our home, from the laneway, the industrial building remains a secret. I was influenced by the city of Tokyo

"Have nothing in your home that you do not know to be useful or believe to be beautiful."

William Morris, textile designer, craftsman, artist, writer, typographer

Back to Basics:
Richard Peters + Heidi Dokulil

_ Focus on the private, unpretentious, and sustainable

_ Find beauty in imperfection

_ Celebrate the handmade over mass-produced

_ Less is more

where land is scarce and buildings are designed to fit onto very small plots of land. We set out to design a new building within the fabric of the old factory. The building shows how much you can achieve in a very small area without compromising space and maintaining the double-height volume of the original building.

"Our old building is new with 21st-century technology that is integrated in our home. It was important to visibly show the history and honesty of the building. We kept the material count low and simply detailed by using unvarnished birch ply, a visible tin roof, and an original exposed brick wall painted in fresh white. Keeping the inside so simple helps Heidi and me unwind when we come inside because there are no visible distractions. We have included only the essential furniture or items we need or have sentimental meaning to us.

"Sustainability was as important to us as having a bathroom. The building has a north-facing roof that has been set up with solar panels to harness the sun, there are operable doors and windows from north to south to allow good cross ventilation so there is no need for air conditioning, while the thermal mass of the concrete floor holds the winter sun to warm the building in the colder months. At night the external lights in the courtyard bounce light back into the building to create a very simple and effective way of reducing the energy needed to illuminate the interior. The ceiling is lined with corrugated steel from the old roof, and a second roof was laid over the top with insulation placed in between."

It's as if many of the middle class have discovered aspiration isn't about having a home that is large, showy and full of bling and are instead focusing on the private, unpretentious, and sustainable.

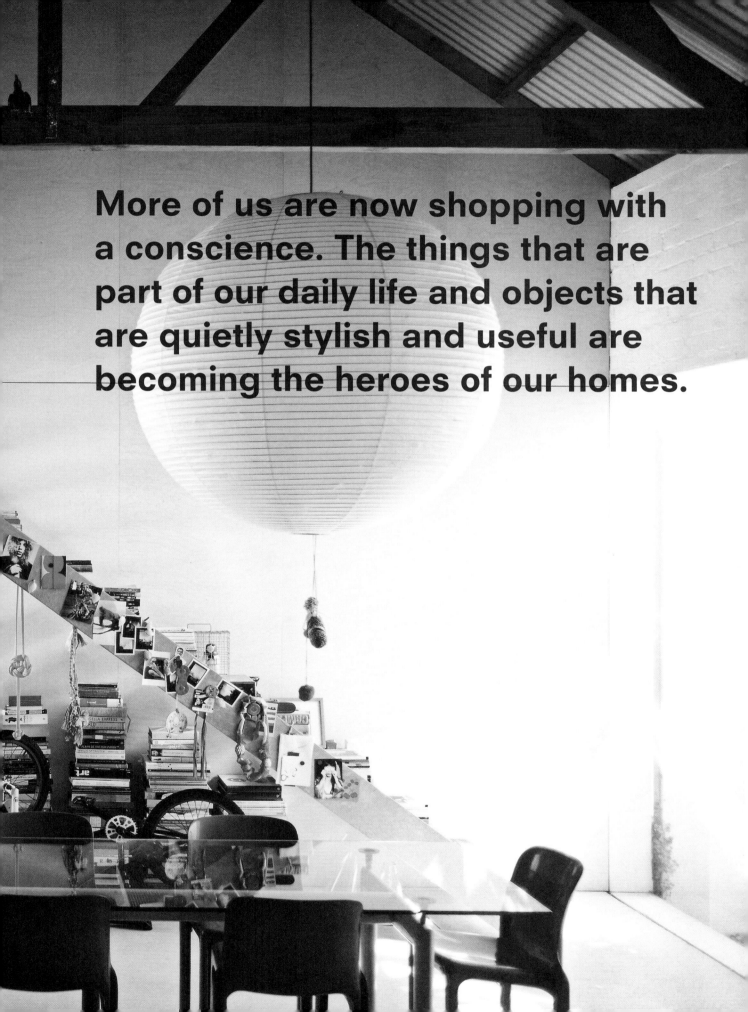

More of us are now shopping with a conscience. The things that are part of our daily life and objects that are quietly stylish and useful are becoming the heroes of our homes.

TOKYO It's important a house gets more beautiful as it ages. Simple and understated unpolished concrete walls are the ideal background for the story of the building's history and will weather with age like a loved leather armchair.

CONCRETE + STONE

INTERNATIONAL TREND
rethink: materials

AKKRUM Exposed concrete floors can be elegant and harmonious. This low-tech, humble, and honest material gives a visual sense of strength and stability, the key need for our homes in these turbulent times.

PARIS Opulence and simplicity manifest in this Paris bathroom by Joseph Dirand architects. Luxurious marble mixed with simple black is the perfect soothing combination for a small bathroom. This calming and serene space is tactile, glamorous, and timeless. The richness in material never interrupts the building's architectural features. A streamlined designed bath and vanity unit keeps an ancient stone modern and fresh.

PARIS The streamlined style and marble detailing conceals functionality, allowing the materials and space to be the hero. SYDNEY Brutal concrete endures effortless and timeless appeal. Pops of vibrant color against cool gray is a match made in heaven.

"What you make
of your life is
up to you.
You have all the
tools and resources
you need.
Your answers lie
inside of you."

Denis Waitley, author and productivity consultant

rethink
create
+ control

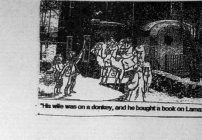

THE OCCUPIED WALL STREET JOURNAL

SATURDAY, OCTOBER 22, 2011

Love Letter to Liberty Square

PEOPLE STEP UP
Bloomberg backs down

5:00 AM FRIDAY—In the day-breaking hours of a long night spent scrubbing and brushing and gardening and packing, a stalwart girl named Julia meticulously swept the tiniest specks from the ground into a dust pan, retracing her steps through Liberty Square again and again.

Occupiers carried boxes to a storage space around the block, and personal stuff was rolled carefully into those ever-present blue tarps, names and phone numbers attached. Preparation of a different sort happened, too: some stayed put and refused to pack up anything.

Two young women, in a subtle and endearing form of protest, sat curled up in blue plastic bins waiting to be carried away. Three hundred people occupied the square.

The day before, Mayor Michael Bloomberg had announced that at 7 a.m., the NYPD would enforce a request by Brookfield Office Properties to clear the park for cleaning. The occupiers, Bloomberg said, would be allowed to return, but many worried that this was a tactic devised to evict the occupation.

A rush of activity commenced. A Facebook page, "Emergency Action: Defend Occupy Wall Street," was forwarded to tens of thousands. Twitter lit up. Emails, text messages and phone calls spread the word. The direct action working group got to it. Organizations everywhere issued statements of support and a unified call for action.

And Occupy Wall Street organizers put out the most urgent call for donations yet: cleaning supplies.

5:30 AM—A line stretched halfway through the park after a mic-checked announcement: coffee had arrived. Following an earlier downpour, clothes were hung to dry on police barricades and twine strung between honey bucket trees. An olive-dressed couple wafted sage

Library was packed into plastic bins and stacked together under a huge blue turtle-shell assembly of tarps. The usual vibrant sprawl of stuff was being consolidated, fortified.

Armaments over shoulder, two occupiers patrolled the north sidewalk. "Preseeeent - mops! March!" Three sentries were on the lookout: a Superman, a Captain America and a Santa Claus. The Sauron-eye of the NYPD mobile observation tower on the northwest corner was, as ever, mostly ignored.

A bottle hurled at a congregation of uniformed and plain-clothed cops across Liberty Street fell ten feet short; they shuffled indoors. An early edition of the Daily News was passed from person to person. The headline: "SHOWDOWN"

6:15 AM—The crowd tripled in ten minutes to well over a thousand. Accredited photographers convened at the trash can bouquet of donated plastic brooms and snapped action shots of occupiers cleaning, now, as performance. On the south side of the square, half a dozen television vans lined up, doors open, video monitors abuzz. Liberty Square neared, then exceeded, capacity.

Mic check: "This special assembly... is now... in session!" Crazy cheers and wiggly fingers from all. "This session is being called for in preparation for the notice that we received, which we know is a pretext, to stop this movement, to silence your voices." The people's mic relayed the message in four concentric waves. "We have two agenda items. The first is briefing from direct action."

From the direct action working group: "We will hold no less than two-thirds of our park at all times. Direct action will be coordinating two lines of non-violent resistance that divide the park in thirds." When it was asked who in the crowd was

OCCUPATION OF TIMES SQUARE: October 15 international day of action brings hundreds of cities around the world into motion. PHOTO: Stephen O'Bryne

OCCUPY YOUR MIND
THE PEOPLE'S LIBRARY

Howard Zinn is here. Dominick Dunne and Tom Wolfe, too. Ernest Hemingway and Barbara Ehrenreich and Dr. Who and Beowulf: All here, and all free. Barnes & Noble may be endangered and the Borders across the street closed months ago, but The People's Library at Liberty Square is open for business and thriving.

That a lending library would spring up fully operational on day one of an occupation makes sense when you consider that the exchange of ideas is paramount here, at a new crossroads of the world. Just as occupiers young and old mingle with Africans, Jews, Algonquins and Latinas, de Tocqueville rubs elbows with Nicholas Evans and Noam Chomsky.

Mandy Henk, 32, saw *Adbusters'* call to occupy Wall Street and drove in from Greencastle, Indiana, on her fall break to work in the library. A librarian at DePaul University,

vanden Heuvel have c and vanden Heuvel h copies of *The Nation*, |

As a result of the become something books. "People are s all over the country out," Syrek said. "We returned."

Volunteers log - aryThing, an online o ning the ISBN app. This bar in "W

AMER

As an awareness of the effect that trade deficits have on governments around the globe and the financial bailouts of big banks increase, so does the mistrust of the general population toward what was the economic status quo.

Faced with insurmountable debts, higher taxes, unattainable property prices, and disappearing pensions, people are feeling increasingly insecure, both financially and emotionally.

Have we lost control of our lives? Fear, resentment, and desperation are now familiar feelings for many of us.

Fed up with being told what to do and how to do it? "Enough is enough" is echoing across the globe. In response, a group of empowered people are taking control, making their own rules to create a sense of stability and security.

Although most of us are living in cities, we are seeking the simple things in life. We seek the imperfections of natural materials, highlighting our thirst for simplicity and honesty. Uncomplicated design that embraces privacy, warmth, clean air, and an abundant source of natural lighting are some of the things we city folk long for.

Stability and security: two things that feel like they are missing in the contemporary world. In the 1960s and 1970s this would have been considered tuning out of society; now it's about getting hands-on with making things and not having to question where or how the product is made. Individuals can gain a sense of being guilt-free by knowing objects that surround them are not coming out of sweatshop factories or impacting the environment. This create-and-control tribe is rediscovering the past, going back to old skills, understanding how objects work and how they are made.

Storytelling and noting the provenance of objects made by hand, along with reclaimed or secondhand objects, is important. There is a revival of the lost skills needed for making objects from scratch, such as building furniture or baking bread, that have been traditionally passed down from generation to generation. The old-fashioned way of creating a sense of "home" is making a comeback. During this unstable time, many individuals have come to the conclusion that they don't need to rely on others to create personal happiness. We have embraced the need to take control of our lives. We have clicked into survival mode— hunger, thirst, and safety have suddenly become our priority. With this determination to take control, people are now prepared to experiment and make things rather than go to the shopping mall to buy things. In doing this, a sense of security is created in our own environment. When I met this new generation of creative pioneers they all expressed the central idea that creating for themselves provides individuality and functionality, as they can customize designs and objects to suit specific needs. Through active involvement in production and handicrafts, we are learning to appreciate traditional ingredients, materials, and methodologies.

"Mass-produced" is becoming a bit of a dirty phrase. People are beginning to question the long-term sustainability of the mass-produced product. Handmade or small-production items are associated with quality, sustainability, well-being, and individuality. It is now important to learn about the provenance of each item you include in your home.

AMERICAN PSYCHIATRIST WILLIAM GLASSER, FOUNDER OF THE INSTITUTE OF REALITY, IDENTIFIED THE FIVE BASIC NEEDS OF ALL HUMAN BEINGS:

1. THE NEED TO SURVIVE AND REPRODUCE.

2. THE NEED TO LOVE AND BELONG.

3. THE NEED FOR (POWER) RECOGNITION.

4. THE NEED FOR FREEDOM OR INDEPENDENCE.

5. THE NEED FOR FUN.

At the start of the recession people were wanting to refocus their life on friends and family instead of social and economic status. But perhaps the fear of loss and failure has made the drive for success more intense.

This brave, creative community has the ability to back away from the materialistic world and think about methods that are deeply considered. The items they are creating and making are not about glamour branding or typography. They're about the essence of humankind—creating.

Recycling, renewing, and reusing are not new ideas but there does seem to be more of us finding creative outlets for making use of handed-down heirlooms, sanding back and repairing furniture, or discovering a secondhand object at a flea market or on eBay to put in our homes. In the past, attempts at using one of the three *R*s weren't considered attractive aesthetics. However, individuals are combining resourcefulness with modern methods, modern technology, and a fresh vision, resulting in amazing and inspiring outcomes for the redesign of our living environment. Things that we make for ourselves, or are made by people or communities we know, have much more personal significance to us.

Domestic industry

Research has shown that people who feel they have some control over situations cope better with stress, are less stressed, and are healthier than people who feel they lack control.

The domestic environment has become a new breeding ground for industry. Entrepreneurs carve out their own optimism by creating items that are imbued with their passion and creative designs.

The new mantra is "Slow down and appreciate methods from the past." Personal creativity is being encouraged by the proliferation of blogs and online markets like Etsy. People are finding time to explore their own creativity—be it knitting or sewing or crafting. People are beginning to question the long-term sustainability of the mass-produced product. Handmade or small-production items are associated with quality, sustainability, well-being, and individuality.

Designers are discovering old handicraft techniques and translating them into a modern environment. Bianca Riggo and Ryan Hanrahan from design firm Page Thirty Three use their home as a studio where they make their products, including the wooden bases for their essential oil burners and bath tonics.

Bianca Riggo and Ryan Hanrahan—Page Thirty Three, Sydney

During the week Tom Tilley is a successful television and radio presenter for ABC. At 1 pm Saturdays at Tom's house in Sydney he has created "Tom Tilley's Mens Cut'n'Convo."

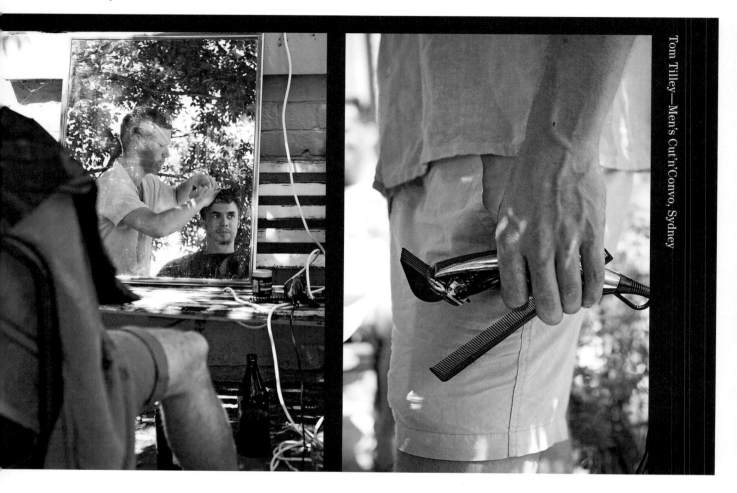

"Bring a longneck, a conversation, and get your hair cut by an amateur hairdresser but professional conversationalist," Tom advertises. His clients range from radio DJs, comedians, and Greenpeace activists who are happy to forgo slick hair salons for a porch, weathered outdoor furniture, and a makeshift mirror. "This is a creative collaboration," explains Tom, "and a free haircut is what makes it attractive to most of my customers."

We're looking for small groups where we can engage in meaningful conversation and to have moments to escape from a technological world.

TEMIKA RIVERA + PATRICK WEDER (Opposite) Both designers and artists based in Brooklyn, Temika and Patrick use their home as a creative hub to make furniture and textiles.

Temika Rivera + Patrick Weder—New York

" It is incredibly satisfying to be industrious at home."

Motivated by a yearning to get back to the basics, Jacqueline Fink carefully crafts beautiful handmade knitted blankets and throws using Australian and New Zealand Merino and Corriedale wools. "I used to live a corporate life as a lawyer. I was unhappy in my job and I wanted to find something I was good at. It was when my mom was very ill and I thought I was going to lose her that my life changed. I used to knit with my mom when I was younger but she used to cast me off on each knitting project. I suddenly realized I needed her to teach me this skill I took for granted because I used to always think, 'Mom will do that.' I flew up to Queensland and she taught me. Since then an addiction started. I knew I wanted to knit chunky knits but I couldn't find the yarn I needed. It took a long search and experiments to find the perfect wool. To work with such a raw natural fiber is a beautiful experience. It's such a tactile material, so there is something incredibly calming when I work with it. Even if I'm stressed out and busy, the minute I sit down and I pick up my wooden needles I am forced to slow down and think. I'm a mom and to be able to work from home producing beautiful throws is a wonderful thing. I sit in the middle of the living room and knit while I can chat to the kids and ask them about their day or keep an eye on them when they are up to some mischief. I work to my schedule so that it fits around my family. It is incredibly satisfying to be industrious at home.

"There is a lot of love put into each throw. To make something with my hands gives me a sense of pride. I know where the wool has come from, I know how many hours have gone into each piece and what was going on in my life when I knitted each throw. It's like they each have their own personalities. I dream that one day people will be able to buy my throws all across the world and they will belong to people who will love them as much as I do. Something I could never say about my old job."

Tired of "sameness" and the push for "standardization," Jacqueline ensures that each piece is a one-of-a-kind creation, something very personal for the user, tactile to handle, textural in its design, and meticulous in its construction.

Jacqueline Fink—Little Dandelion, Sydney

FRIDAY, APRIL 22, 2005

TELL THE TRUTH

Inez Valk-Kempthorne and Justus Kempthorne—Bloomville, New York

Creating a different space for living

As a result of the global economic upheaval, people are opting for an aesthetic of simplicity, harking back to "better times."

There is an emphasis on doing things for less, both with materials and finances. Inez Valk-Kempthorne and Justus Kempthorne are a couple who are literally living "the good life" in New York.

Inez and Justus have lived in vibrant cities such as Amsterdam and New York. Inez was a successful model and Justus is a carpenter. They wanted to simplify their lives and live in a healthy environment. They built and own their home outright, no trust fund involved, and have opted for a self-sustaining lifestyle that minimizes economic stress. The city of New York is close enough to visit but far enough away to allow them to live a life in the "country."

Justus outlines their overarching philosophy: "We don't have faith in the government, so we wanted to take control in our own lives and create our own security and stability. We didn't want to live in fear. We wanted to live in an environment filled with kindness. We are starting a local (food) cafe and wood shop in the town of Bloomville."

"Our lives have changed dramatically since we moved away from the city and built our own home in the middle of nature. When you move to the country that [high-tempo city] beat slows down and changes into something different. Less like a train about to crash. The country is much less stressful," says Inez.

"We lived fully off the grid for a few years with a solar panel for lights and charging batteries, a propane refrigerator, a composting toilet, and a gravity-fed water system for dishes and cold, cold baths in the pond! It was amazing to become so aware of the impact we have on the world and also realize how easily humans can adapt," says Justus.

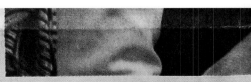

Love
Liber

PEO
Bloom

5:00 AM FRIDAY—
breaking hours of
spent scrubbing and
gardening and pack
girl named Julia met
the tiniest specks fro
into a dust pan, retr
through Liberty Squ
again.

Occupiers carrie
storage space arou
and personal stuff
fully into those ev
tarps, names and phone numbers
attached. Preparation of a different
sort happened, too: some stayed put
and refused to pack up anything.

Two young women, in a subtle
and endearing form of protest, sat
curled up in blue plastic bins waiting to be carried away. Three hun-

as ever, mostly ignored.

A bottle hurled at a congregation
of uniformed and plain-clothed
cops across Liberty Street fell ten
feet short; they shuffled indoors. An
early edition of the Daily News was
passed from person to person. The
headline: "SHOWDOWN"

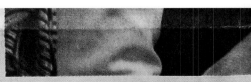
OCCUPATION OF TIMES SQUARE: October 15 international

"His wife was on a donkey, and he bought a book on Lamaze."

DELHI!

ETVILLE!

SUE 3

undreds of cities around the world into motion. PHOTO: Stephen O'Bryne

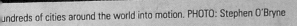

"Our home is not designed, it is formed by the materials we found. We built our home mainly from reclaimed materials and rough-cut timber from local sawmills. We love to 'dumpster dive' and give abandoned materials a second life. Because of this choice we were able to stay out of debt when we built our home.

"We think it is very important to realize the impermanence of everything. We are very happy with the home we built but knowing it could be swept away in some new megastorm or blasted with a solar flare and burn back to the earth is okay, too."

Individuals across the globe are identifying with Inez and Justus a need to escape from jobs that give little fulfillment and cities inundated with rules and regulations for their idea of utopia.

"We don't have
faith in the government,
so we wanted to
take control in
our own life and
create our own
security and stability.
We didn't want to
live in fear."

Justus Kempthorne, New York

OWNER: ANETTE HOLMBERG
LOCATION: SKABELONLOFTET, COPENHAGEN, DENMARK

Control isn't a need, it is a function to fulfill our needs. Our lives are a continual struggle to gain control in a way that will satisfy our needs and not deprive those around us, especially those close to us.

In Copenhagen there stands a rundown shipyard that was derelict before painter Anette Holmberg discovered it. "The old Burmeister and Wain shipyard had been vacant for years but when I came to visit this rustic building I could instantly see the potential," explains Anette. "It can be lonely being an artist, so I wanted to build a creative community around me in an inspiring space."

She has created a professional creative community in the enormous 15,070-square-foot/1,400-square-meter warehouse. "The aim was to

create a place where a mixture of commercial, artistic, and innovative forces can meet and interact with each other." Anette has filled the space with seventeen studios shared among fifty-two tenants who are a mixture of architects, artists, designers, set builders, and journalists. "In a world where we feel increasingly divorced from the people around us, there's a yearning for community," she says.

Each of her tenants are shown the space they can occupy but it is up to them to build their own walls and interiors. Anette's studio is vast, allowing her to hang her large canvases and paint freely. She has built herself a cozy nook, including a kitchen and seating area to sit and enjoy a coffee or relax with her laptop on a worn leather chair.

"I knew I could change the mind-set in giving way to the fatalistic attitude about this old shipyard to a sense of longing for something better—and, equally important, a belief that it could be achieved." Anette Holmberg, Copenhagen

Create + Control: Anette Holmberg

_ Taking matters into her own hands

_ Reviving old skills needed to make objects from scratch

_ Recycling, reusing, and reinventing

_ Encouraging personal creativity over mass production

_ Bringing a community together who share the same values and ideas

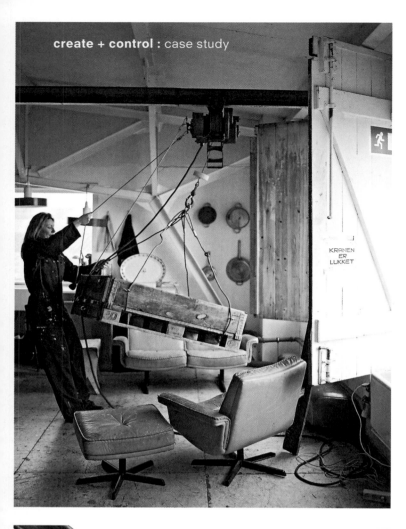

"I'm certainly not frightened of an electric drill anymore. I love coming here to my space, throwing on my overalls, and being in the world I have created for myself."

Anette's creative hub has sparked an interest in the area. An area that had become a ghost town is now seeing a growth in property values because of its newfound popularity with businesses and artists. "By sharing with friends and neighbors, we become connected as communities, enjoying shared endeavors. Empowering each other, creating shared moral values, and tackling local problems including crime and youth disfranchisement," says Anette.

Anette now receives visits from her government and other foreign governments to learn how to turn barren industrial areas into thriving community hubs.

With thriving cities short of housing, it is an exciting prospect to think that individuals are seeing the value of underused buildings and neighborhoods. Combining business and creative hubs creates a very positive future.

"This project has served a purpose: it has helped me pursue sacred modern values—individual freedom, personal control, and self-realization. By sharing with friends and neighbors, we become connected as communities, enjoying shared endeavors."

COPENHAGEN **You can be positive that you can make your home into something special and uniquely yours by being inventive. Old disused nautical charts from a booming shipyard are now reinvented into charming doors. A recycled, toughened cardboard canister formerly used to store Kodak film is now conveniently reused as a multifunctional bedside table and storage unit for odds and ends.**

INTERNATIONAL TREND
rethink: materials

RE-USE
RE-INVENT
RE-CYCLE

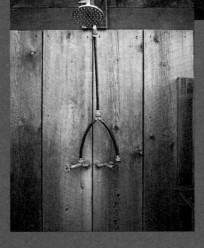

NEW YORK **It can be really rewarding to find pieces for nothing and turn them into something. Look out for old wood offcuts, floorboards, or fencing. They offer a warm, organic look while making efficient use of this precious resource.**

COPENHAGEN The obvious is not always the way to go. The only limit is your imagination when it comes to what you can upcycle. Magazine tear sheets can be a great addition to a boring kitchen counter, and an old vacuum cleaner dust filter can be transformed into an industrial light.

SYDNEY Find and choose objects that encapsulate your personal story. Learn about the provenance of each item you include in your home. Flea markets are an ideal place to find affordable artwork and frames for your home. You never know, you may grab a masterpiece.

LONDON Everything can be repurposed. Unwanted tea chests are a savvy storage solution for any style of home. They are a warm and unpretentious addition to a bedroom or living room as bedside or side tables. Adding a modern light is a great way to turn what could have been trash into desirable furniture.

"People are increasingly concerned about how their food has been manipulated and processed, genetic modification, the distance food travels before reaching their plates, and many other related issues."

Clive van Heerden, senior director, Phillips Design

rethink
self-sufficient
living

A trend emerging in overpopulated cities is urban farms within the home. For some people it's a simple pleasure, a new hobby. But many others are part of a fast-growing tribe of people becoming local producers and taking hold of the mantra "local, not global." It is not hard to believe that with an ever-expanding interest in different varieties of produce and the growing process, many people have decided to produce food for themselves within their home and their local community.

This tribe of people aren't from any specific age group, socioeconomic background, or country; and they're not laid-back hessian-dressed hippies who want to drop out of society. These people simply demand quality food that tastes delicious, is grown sustainably with a low environmental impact, and is not treated with harmful chemicals.

Eagle Street Rooftop community farm located in Brooklyn, New York, is one of many urban renewal projects popping up across the globe. The produce grown on top of the 6000-square-foot/557-square-meter warehouse rooftop is sold to neighbors, local suppliers, and restaurants. This initiative provides opportunities for community members to be directly involved in growing the produce they buy.

BIG IDEAS: AMAZING THINGS HAPPENING

Growing productive crops from balconies, stairwells, indoor gardens, window boxes, and rooftops.

Fish farming at home.

Beekeeping in urban cities.

Poultry farming in backyards and balconies.

SMALL IDEAS: HOW YOU CAN ADAPT THEM

Plant things you love to eat to encourage you to take care of what you are growing. Creatively think about how to use space in your home to have a small garden.

Do some research into the types of farm animals that are okay to have in an urban environment, such as chickens, ducks, or pigs.

From tomatoes growing from window ledges in Brixton, United Kingdom, to a little kitchen in Sydney, Australia, farming fish and entire rooftops in New York City being used for commercial farming, it's becoming crystal clear we are finding ways to grow and gather our own food in an urban environment. Making the most of our window boxes and roof gardens not only saves at the supermarket checkout; it feeds our nostalgia for the "good life"—an idyllic time when food was seasonal and locally sourced.

Apart from the feel-good factor, the urban farm movement has a wider impact in helping with the future of our cities. As the world population continues to grow and our cities expand, food shortage is one of the big issues many of us will face. By 2050, 70 percent of the world's population will be living in urban cities and thus urban farming will become a significant and necessary factor for food production.

Scientists are predicting that for our children's generation food shortage is a strong possibility. By 2050, the world's population will swell to more than nine billion. At the moment the global head-count is sitting at seven billion.

The urgent task that world governments need to tackle is feeding an ever-growing population with diminishing resources. It is estimated that a 70 percent increase in food production will be needed to feed the global population. As much as 50 percent of the world's population already live in an urban sprawl and this number is expected to rise to 70 percent in the next forty years. This is why it is encouraging to see so many people and communities in cities becoming self-sufficient with farming and local producers.

It amazes me the amount of plants local councils plant each year. My dream is that these plants are replaced with edible ones, providing free food for local residents.

Farmers' markets are becoming mainstream in busy cities. Urban residents are turning to local produce. A growing number of consumers prefer to buy fresh, locally grown produce for superior quality and flavor of food. Farmers' markets provide consumers with the opportunity to connect with the producers, learn about their produce and their passion, and witness firsthand how this enthusiasm translates into superior quality.

TODAY, 49 PERCENT OF THE WORLD'S POPULATION LIVE IN CITIES

800 MILLION PEOPLE ARE INVOLVED IN URBAN AGRICULTURE WORLDWIDE AND CONTRIBUTE TO FEEDING URBAN RESIDENTS

LOW-INCOME URBAN DWELLERS SPEND BETWEEN 40 PERCENT AND 60 PERCENT OF THEIR INCOME ON FOOD EACH YEAR

BY 2015, ABOUT 26 CITIES IN THE WORLD ARE EXPECTED TO HAVE A POPULATION OF 10 MILLION OR MORE

TO FEED A CITY OF THIS SIZE AT LEAST 6,600 TONS/6,000 METRIC TONNES OF FOOD MUST BE IMPORTED AND SUPPLIED EACH DAY

AT THE MOMENT, 250 MILLION HUNGRY PEOPLE IN THE WORLD LIVE IN CITIES

Small steps in how we use unused spaces in our cities have become more important to local communities. Edible gardens are being introduced to encourage community engagement as well as providing places for people to relax. Sam Crawford Architects in Sydney, Australia, and Joost Bakker, a Dutch artist based in Melbourne, are just some of the pioneers who are showing affordable and inventive solutions.

Isn't it amazing that cooking from scratch has become a trend? Especially when this is what our grandparents did daily until ready-made meals and processed foods became the norm. Cooking from scratch is about using quality ingredients; simple, honest food cooked from the heart. Celebrity chefs, governments, and campaigners are encouraging the trend, not only for a healthy lifestyle but to cut down on food waste.

The other major factor to stop food waste is climate change. According to the International Food Policy Research Institute, a 1.8°F/1°C increase in global temperature over the next forty years could mean a 30 to 100 percent increase in the cost of food. Food prices are set to rise 15 to 45 percent over the next decade according to the Organisation for Economic Co-Operation and Development and the United Nations Food and Agriculture Organization.

Americans throw away more than a third of the food they buy, totaling more than four hundred dollars worth of food a year per person. The food industry produces about 4 tons/3.6 metric tonnes in total (compared to 8 tons/7.2 metric tonnes from households), and within that only around 0.4 tons/0.4 metric tonnes comes from supermarkets.

INTERNATIONAL TREND
rethink: harvest

NEW YORK **Often when you grow your own food you will have a bumper crop. Instead of wasting food, individuals are preserving their harvest. It's one of the oldest forms of keeping food for the winter months when stocks run low. Making homemade jams, chutneys, and pickles, and drying out herbs and spices are just a few ways to make sure your food lasts.**

COPENHAGEN It's not always about growing on a big scale. You can see individuals growing herbs and vegetables on their sunny windowsills. It may not feed your family on a large scale but it certainly gives the sense of satisfaction in knowing you have grown something from scratch. Seeing something grow certainly plays on the nostalgic feeling for the "good life."

CHICAGO Growing your own mini herb garden and having a constant supply of fresh leaves to flavor favorite dishes is the biggest and most common trend we are seeing in kitchens across the globe. Many herbs are easy to grow from seed. Recycle your eggshells and use them as planters to sow your seeds.

After watching celebrity chef and campaigner Hugh Fearnley-Whittingstall's *Fish Fight*, which championed a neglected cause—the sustainable use of fish from the seas and the misleading labeling supermarkets are providing on their packaging—it's not surprising to find a rumbling of people farming their own fish to eat.

We may start seeing "Pond to Plate" on restaurant menus. I believe new-build apartment blocks could integrate aquaponics into the buildings, providing vegetables and fish to the residents who live in them.

Designers are looking at how we can humanely breed and keep edible fish at home. Philips Design created a prototype, The Food Probe, which is a biosphere home farm containing fish, crustaceans, algae, plants, and other mini-ecosystems, all interdependent and in balance with each other. The fish also benefit from this process, as the water is filtered by the plants, giving the fish clean water to live in. Aquaponics uses less water to produce the same amount of food as conventional agriculture, organic agriculture, and hydroponics. It means both fish and plants survive as a result of each other

This is commonly called aquaponics. An aquaponic system uses the water from the fish tank to circulate through a grow bed where the plants are grown. Nitrifying bacteria converts fish wastes into plant-available nutrients. The plants use these nutrients as their main nutrient supply. and you don't have to tend to them as much as a typical edible garden. Perfect for people who live in cities who are time-poor. Young designers in Europe are trying to develop some good-looking aquaponics because some of the commercial stuff out there isn't very pretty.

"My next-door neighbor
has lived on our street
since World War II and
tells me how it was really
common practice for people
in London to breed pigs in
their backyard during the
war years for food."

Antonia Pugh-Thomas, London

Residential and community producers

A resurging interest in where our food comes from is the driving force behind people wanting to grow more of it themselves.

Growing numbers of individuals are nervous to eat food from supermarkets since commercial food producers commonly use practices such as battery hens, chemicals to create flavor, and genetically modified vegetables. While governments debate the safety of these types of food production, 67 percent of the produce sold in America is genetically modified.

Homegrown produce always tastes better than store-bought produce. Not only that, there is an increasing distrust of big chain supermarkets who are using their buying power to push for high-yield food production in order to set lower prices for their customers. In the short term, this has sent small-yield producers out of business. In the long term, this large-scale food production is unsustainable in terms of the drain on the land and it also diminishes good farming practices that are sustainable.

People want to know where their food comes from and consumer groups are actively campaigning for this information to be available at point of sale so consumers know if something is locally produced. Why eat an apple that could have been stored up to ten months before it hits the supermarket or be forced to buy fish that has been transported from miles away?

"'Salmon has to be smoked,' my grandfather used to say. 'Carry on regardless.' I guess I am just following his footsteps, from the north of Norway all the way down to North London."

Ole Martin Hansen,
Hansen & Lydersen, London

With the supermarket chains' hunger for growing profits, they have created a throwaway culture to encourage their customers to continue buying more from them. Despite large volumes of food being sold in supermarkets, 98.1 million tons/89 million metric tonnes of food is wasted each year in the European Union (EU). Up to 50 percent of edible and healthy food is wasted in EU households, supermarkets, restaurants, and along the food supply chain right through to consumer consumption. The United Kingdom, America, and Australia are all guilty of unforgivable amounts of wasted food. Food is no longer a precious commodity. The quest for self-sufficiency is also a reaction to this throwaway culture that pervades first-world societies.

We are being encouraged to bring the homegrown back into our daily life. With the increased concern about where our food comes from, "growing your own" gives families the opportunity to be self-sufficient as much as they can.

Urban farming increases the amount of fresh food, such as vegetables, fruit, and meat, available to people living in highly populated cities. The present state of affairs may sound bleak but if we use the resources available to us cleverly, we city dwellers can create a bright future. Emerging urban tribes are starting a powerful green revolution. From neglected urban wastelands to high-rise apartment balconies, these spaces are being transformed into edible gardens. More green space also means cleaner air and a habitat for wildlife.

When researching urban local producers I used Twitter to ask if anyone knew of any bee, chicken, or pig farmers. It was clear from the rapid and vast response there is a buzz for urban beekeeping. From rooftops and backyards to community gardens, urban beehives are becoming more common across the globe. The honeybee is under threat from a deadly parasite known as *Verroa destructor* and colony collapse disorder. Urban beekeepers are doing their bit to save bees from becoming an endangered species.

The common bond that was so obvious when meeting global urban farmers and producers was that they all had one passion—quality produce. Talking to them about what they were nurturing and growing was similar to the heartfelt conversation you have with a new parent. They're not caught up a current fad, they simply love what they do and they know they're creating a healthier life for their family and community. To me, they are all artisans. "Authenticity," "integrity," "providence," and "sustainability" are words that belong to all of our new farming pioneers.

"Keeping bees is a way of feeling connected to the bigger picture of the environment and helping out in a small way. Bees seem to be as happy in the city, if not happier, as they don't mind pollution, but hate pesticides and most gardeners don't use them in the city."

Chantal Coady,
Rococo Chocolates, London

OWNER: RONNIE HUDGELL
LOCATION: LONDON, UK

When we walk around the food aisles in supermarkets we are offered so much choice. Well, we think we are. When I visited a French supermarket I was amazed to see how many different varieties of chickens there are. Such a contrast to my local supermarket in Australia. Being a city girl I only knew my chickens by breast, leg, thigh, and wing.

So much of the food we eat comes from overseas. It's hard not to ask questions about how sustainably our local region can supply food to locals. It's amazing though if you start to look in your local streets what you can find.

In a little back garden attached to a terraced house in Newham, East London, seventeen-year-old Ronnie Hudgell has turned his mom and dad's backyard into a poultry farm.

"I have noticed a growing interest in people wanting to own poultry. I think more people want to eat their own fresh eggs and have them as pets for their children," Ronnie says.

Ronnie started being a poultry farmer at thirteen when a lady responding to an advertisement he posted on the Internet sent him seventy quail eggs and an incubator. From these he was able to hatch forty-five quails. "It was really an amazing moment to see my first quail hatch. From that moment I was hooked and from then on I tried to hatch everything. I even gave an ostrich and emu egg a go," says Ronnie.

Ronnie has proved this has not just been a hobby but a small business. This business has even caught the attention of Jamie Oliver.

"Young professionals are buying quails from me for their balconies to have fresh eggs in the morning."

Quail eggs used to be considered a delicacy in many countries. With a new global fascination in cooking this little egg it's now becoming more popular and easier to find. A quail will lay approximately two eggs a day for her whole life. Full of protein and vitamin D, the quail egg is rumored to stimulate growth, increase sexual appetite, and stimulate brain functions. Not bad for this delicious, creamy egg.

Self-Sufficient Living: Ronnie Hudgell
_ Demanding quality in food
_ Providing fresh and local produce to an urban community
_ Helping to cut down on food waste
_ Sustainable farming practices
_ Knowing the provenance of the food

TOKYO Kitchens need to be robust, honest, and equipped to work hard. Smart design at an appetizing price is the trend. Kitchens that help householders to reuse and recycle as much as possible are on the up.

AMSTERDAM Food and how we eat isn't just about the ingredients. Increasingly we seek out local artisans creating classic and regional tableware.

INTERNATIONAL TREND
rethink: materials

EASY-ACCESS KITCHENS

PARIS Today's kitchen isn't about glossy, sleek, white units and gadgets. More of us desire a working country kitchen. We want more room to store our fresh produce and have easy access to our cooking utensils. Combining materials and accessories that personalize the space allows the kitchen to sit well in its environment.

<u>NEW YORK</u> Kitchens are now being designed as living spaces where nature and technology are seamlessly integrated. Studio Gorm's Flow 2 Kitchen incorporates an organic cycle where food is grown, stored, cooked, and composted. <u>LONDON</u> Wood adds warmth and individuality to the hub of the home. There has been a rise in cultivation cabinets and cupboards in which young plants can be grown and food can be stored.

<u>SYDNEY</u> With more of us wanting to cook from scratch, kitchen design focuses on creating functional and approachable spaces that feature modern conveniences while avoiding the homogeneous aesthetic of the showroom kitchen.

"Our houses are no longer simply homes but where we work, study, socialize, and shop. We demand dwellings that celebrate the rituals of domestic life and allow for privacy and a change of mood."

Amanda Talbot

rethink

ever-changing

space

With technology becoming smarter, the notion of a "room" for a specific purpose is changing. Designers are trying to integrate technology into everyday life so that it becomes invisible. Product design is becoming like architecture. Design is becoming "invisible" as digital devices shrink the world of industrial design.

There is an evolution going on inside the home. On one side of the coin, we want items and objects that evoke emotion. With technology becoming more interactive, intuitive, and integrated, items including televisions, traditional lighting, even bookshelves will be objects more commonly designated to landfill rather than making a statement in the home.

With the products of industrial design shrinking in size, what once took up space in the home is no longer doing so.

We want our technology to be seamless with the architecture of our home. Unsightly cables will be a thing of the past as our homes become "smarter" and wireless. Parisian architect Joseph Dirand has hidden all of his cabling for his speakers and other electronic devices in this multifunctional hollow floating concrete bench. The owners also use the bench to sit on and display loved possessions.

Shelves for CDs and DVDs are becoming a thing of the past. Traditional zones, such as bedrooms, kitchens, and lounge rooms are becoming blurred and the house space is becoming more flexible, reflecting how a family interacts in the frame of the living environment. The frame, or as some like to call it, the "shell," of the home may not change but inside this frame, families of today are using space rather than the space imposing itself on the family. Phillips Design Hub, headquartered in Eindhoven, has been exploring future landscapes of interaction between people and new technologies. Spaces for relaxing, reading, working, and devouring media are now being integrated into all areas of the house. With integrated technology in the home ranging from smart walls to touch-top kitchen stovetops to LED fabrics, questions are being asked as to how a modern room should be designed and function.

Open shelving

Open shelving is a simple form of changing the function of a room. The shelves used to hold books, entertainment equipment, and mementos can be changed easily.

Pods are the perfect solution in giving the residents privacy in an open-plan studio space. When doors are closed it helps block out noise and light but when doors are slid open an individual can socialize and feel connected with their family. Mobile walls give an open space more living flexibility and are a great storage unit to hide the kids' toys.

People can get the sense that a space is bigger if they can't figure out the size of it. By obscuring views and giving the impression that a maze of doorways, platforms, enclosed rooms, and overhangs go on and on, design trickery provides the feeling of privacy and space and flexibility for the family.

MULTIFUNCTIONAL ROOM

IN HOMES WHERE SPACE IS AT A PREMIUM IT IS
NECESSARY TO HAVE ROOMS AND FURNITURE
THAT CAN BE MULTIFUNCTIONAL. OUR HOMES
NOW DEMAND A MORE EFFECTIVE USE OF
SPACE. A MULTIFUNCTIONAL ROOM CAN
ACCOMMODATE TWO OR MORE ACTIVITIES
EITHER SIMULTANEOUSLY OR ALTERNATELY.
EACH AREA NEEDS TO SWITCH BETWEEN FAMILY
REQUIREMENTS AND GUEST REQUIREMENTS.
FOR EXAMPLE:

KITCHEN = COOKING/EATING/PANTRY/FARMING/
SHOPPING/SOCIAL

BEDROOM = SLEEP/WORKING/ENTERTAINMENT/
SHOPPING/PRIVACY

LIVING ROOM = ENTERTAINMENT/LOUNGING/
SOCIAL/PRIVACY/EATING/WORKING/SHOPPING

BATHROOM = CLEANING/BATHING/MEDIA/PRIVACY

NOOKS FOR PRIVACY
In the communal areas of the house where family members come together to socialize and eat, open spaces have replaced separate, tiny rooms. Room dividers made from fabric or glass are commonly used to divide dining, study, living, bedrooms, and bathrooms. Often quiet spaces for adults are created by a screen or nook for a family member to escape from the communal hub of the house.

INTERNATIONAL TREND
rethink: floor space

SYDNEY Beds are big and they take up a lot of floor space. Anthony Gill Architects have installed a queen-size bed into this studio apartment that can be pulled out when it is time to go to sleep and hidden away during the day. When designing the drawer make sure you leave enough room to slide an unmade bed away.

AMSTERDAM The key to keeping your floor clear from clutter is storage, storage, storage. When it comes to small spaces a wall of floor-to-ceiling cupboards can be overbearing. Architects i29 have turned what could have been a very white and bland apartment into a showstopper featuring a series of cabinets with laser-cut holes that double as handles.

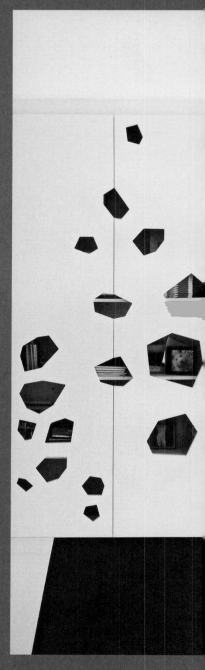

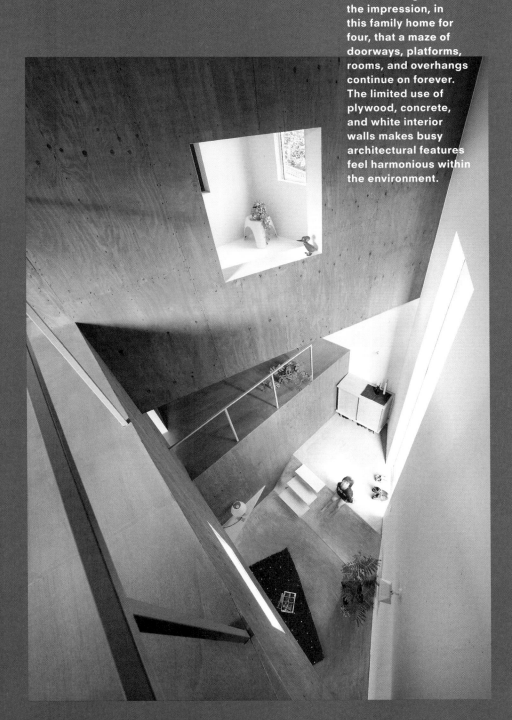

HIROSHIMA Make a space feel larger by obscuring views of each room and floor within the home. Japanese architects Suppose Design Office have given the impression, in this family home for four, that a maze of doorways, platforms, rooms, and overhangs continue on forever. The limited use of plywood, concrete, and white interior walls makes busy architectural features feel harmonious within the environment.

Yuko Shibata—Tokyo, Japan

Home as a living puzzle

Clever design converts and changes according to need.

With housing in cities across the world becoming more dense we are leaning toward the Japanese way of living. Japanese homes are famous for their flexibility of space; the interior of a room can be altered for different occasions by using screens and furniture to have the same sort of flexibility. Japanese designer Yuko Shibata created separate living and working areas by installing mobile walls in her one-bedroom Tokyo apartment. "When we have visitors they are always amazed at how flexible our house is. They love how it transforms into a home to an office and back into a home," says Yuko.

For most of us, the notion of working from home isn't too much of a sacrifice because we have space but in Tokyo apartments are small. When Yuko first saw the apartment she thought it was impossible to transform it into a multifunctional space.

The house has become a living puzzle as a result of it having many different uses and accommodating a range of people. The home now needs to be able to allow the occupier to swap and change activities with ease." The addition of two bookshelves in the apartment, each with a large door, allowed us to create a space with the ability to adapt from home to office or from office to home, while leaving the original floor plan intact," says Yuko.

"I have called this apartment 'Switch.'
I work from my apartment during the day but when
my partner comes home in the evening we can slide
the wall back and turn my office into our space."

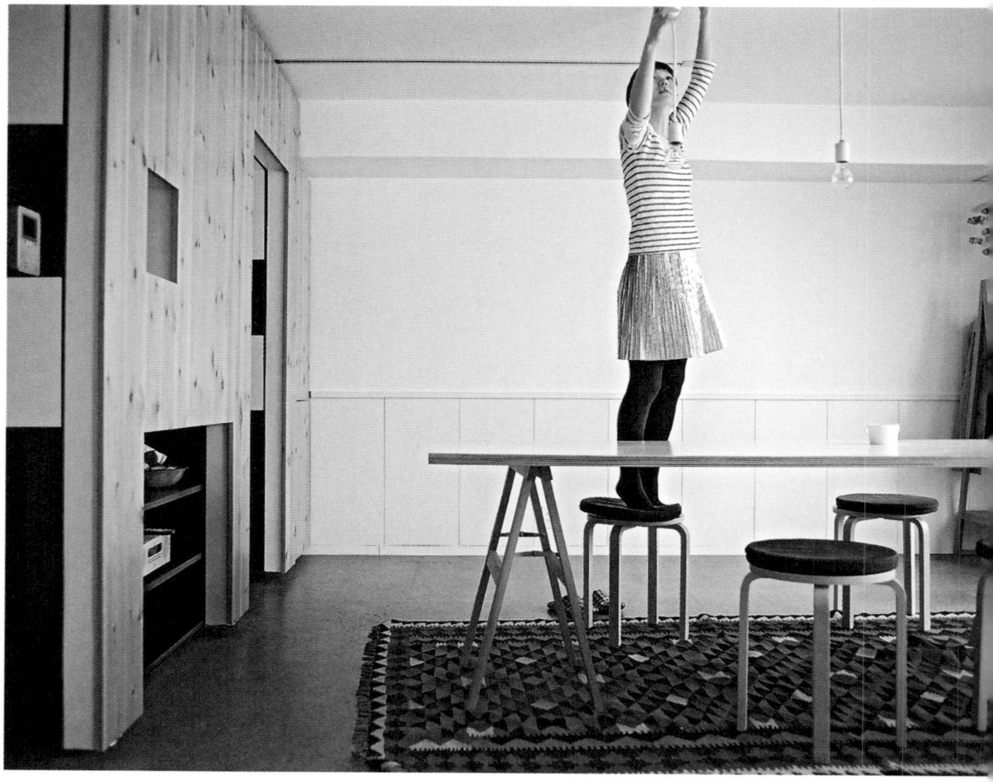

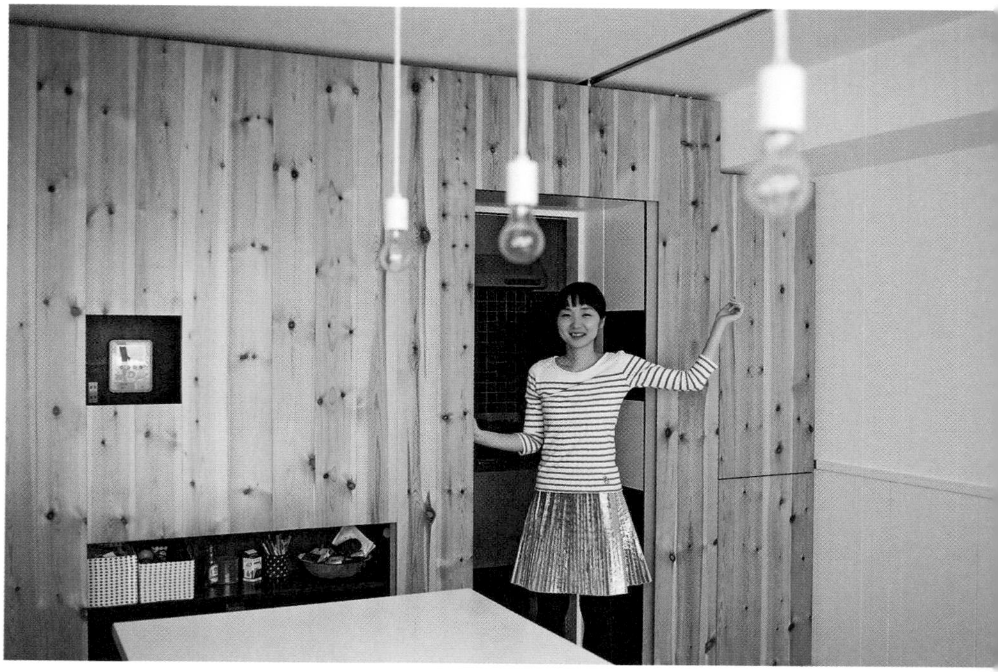

Yuko has called the apartment "Switch." In the front room one partition slides out over the dining table to create a meeting room on one side and library on the other. In the main living area the first bookshelf was added to the meeting room. By moving the large door, the meeting space can be divided in two. "In Japan people work long hours, so the time we need our space to function as a home is very little," explains Yuko. "It's empowering to be able to select how we want to use the space. When I want to concentrate I will slide the wall to be in the black library. When I want to be inspired or consider a new idea I choose to be in the meeting room."

A second bookcase holding books and paperwork and loved objects pivots to reveal a bedroom at the end of the day.

It's about solutions for the family who lives in a given space. They have the basic structure, but then the rest fits their lifestyle.

When living in a small space it can be overwhelming. The lack of privacy, storage, and even trying to keep it looking neat and tidy are big challenges. It's very easy to look at your next-door neighbor who might have a bigger house and feel envious. Yuko shows that by rethinking her living space it is possible to adjust and reconfigure even the smallest of areas for little money. What it does take is some creative thinking and understanding how you want to live in your home.

Don't let an original layout dictate how you live because it can constantly keep changing to the way you live.

"In Japan we work
long hours, so the time
we need our space to
function as a home is
very little. It's empowering
to be able to select
how we want to use
the space."

OWNERS: BRITT CREPAIN + STEFAN SPAENS
LOCATION: ANTWERP, BELGIUM

This house is built on a very small plot of land that is 13 feet/4 meters wide by 50 feet/15 meters deep in the center of Antwerp. The house itself measures 13 feet/4 meters by 39 feet/ 12 meters. Such a tiny footprint meant that Britt had to be clever when designing her home, making sure she made the most of every available centimeter. The clever solution was to build up five floors. The biggest challenge of living in such a narrow space was to make sure there was plenty of natural light, so she installed skylights above the stairwells and a glass front façade.

Another challenge of using such a small space was not only creating privacy but making the house facilitate the interaction of the people living there. To achieve this Britt and Stefan organized each space on split levels. There is plenty of privacy in the house

with nooks tucked away but at the same time the spaces are very social.

As Britt says, "When I'm in the kitchen I can interact with others in the dining room or in the library or I can view down the void created by the staircase and talk easily to anyone in the house."

"The interior colors and materials used are as natural as possible. Our home breathes calmness and serenity." Britt and Stefan are inspired by the colors they found on a beach in Camargue, France, on a sunny day. The beach colors from the sand, the pebbles, and the driftwood bleached by the sea formed a beautiful atmosphere. "We wanted this in our home. We have used natural lime stucco for the walls, the floors are in wood-casted concrete, a polyurethane flooring, and all the fixed-furniture is made of birch multiplex."

"My home is not a traditional home and has had to fit into my life, routine, and the small plot of land I live on. It is light and gives me room to have privacy."

Ever-Changing Space:
Britt Crepain + Stefan Spaens

_ Nooks for privacy have been created

_ The rooms are multifunctional

_ Technology and lighting have been integrated

_ Using the space rather than the space imposing itself on the family

You never know where life
unexpected ways. A home

Much thought went into the use of technology in the house. "I have seamlessly integrated the technology in our home. I have selected key task lighting including a pendant hanging above the dining table but the main lighting for the home is tucked in between the storage cupboards and concrete ceilings throughout. One of my favorite designs in my home is the washroom hidden behind the bookshelf in my reading room. When visitors come to visit for the first time they always smile when I tell them to just open the bookcase. My home is not a traditional home and has had to fit into my life, routine, and the small plot I live on. It could have easily been a depressing, dark home; it is anything but. It is light and friendly and gives me room to have privacy without ever feeling lonely," explains Britt. Sometimes life unfolds in unexpected ways. Britt has created not only a home for her and her partner but one that will expand, adjust, and be the perfect background when she has a family. You can't change the size of the house but you can make the most of the space. A rooftop can be a spectacular substitute for a garden where you can entertain. Enhance the space with light-weight furniture so it's not too hard to get up there and move around.

can take you. Sometimes life unfolds in
needs to be flexible for those moments.

"The essence of optimism is that it is a source of inspiration, of vitality, and hope where others have resigned; it enables a man to hold his head high, to claim the future for himself, and not to abandon it to his enemy."

Dietrich Bonhoeffer, theologian, spiritual writer, and martyr

rethink

optimistic
design

design

We are pushing aside the gloom of climate change, shortages of natural resources, and the endless media stories making us feel guilty about everything. We are taking control and making our new world better by simply dictating how we want to live.

Optimistic design isn't a particular look, it is a movement of residential anarchy. It goes much deeper than using bright colors—it's an attitude displaying self-empowerment, nurturing a more upbeat approach to living. It is about doing things differently, to kick against what is currently on-trend. The only guiding principle is that there is no guiding principle.

It is a crusade where a new breed of self-curating, design-smart amateurs who blog about their rebellious design have led the way. They have coined the word "undecorate."

More people are finding freedom of expression and a playful approach in design. Emmanuelle Moureaux Architecture & Design have designed a bank in Tokiwadai, Tokyo, with recessed brightly colored windows. The outside of buildings can be a powerful approach to help lift the mood of stressed-out city residents.

They are proud of their home and they are not going to hide it just because it doesn't belong in traditional interior magazines. Because of the ripples of the global financial crisis, these new self-made designers are spurred on by resourcefulness.

Using the Internet, they're finding discounted materials and furnishings and the result is an outpouring of home-grown inventiveness—sofas upholstered with hessian coffee sacks, vacuum cleaners made into lights, party decorations used as permanent decoration. For the moment, these novices have upstaged the experts and have become the authorities. The one thing we can take from this rough-edged amateur movement is that real life is in flux.

Polished design is passé. Think textures, history, and bold colors. Torn wallpaper and paint smeared across interior walls is the greatest example of all rules being broken in traditional interior design. Our amateur and rebellious designers are wanting to create a personal story on every surface in the home, including the walls. A space feeling worn rather than polished gives us a sense of history. It's not about bringing in the professional tradesmen but having a go and being free to express yourself.

The so-called style gurus often demand that we undergo a form of de-narration, a term coined by novelist Douglas Coupland. Our optimistic design pioneers are not interested in stripping the home back to its unlived state but embracing Coupland's philosophy of de-narration, "the process whereby one's life stops feeling like a story." In relation to the style gurus, this means adopting the purely personal regardless of external influences.

WALL ART TRENDS
Lack of money is no barrier with this trend. Homeowners are creating their own works of art filled with humor. From empty frames being painted and grouped together to simply using tape to haphazardly display family photographs, the display of art is an optimistic, juvenile approach that individuals don't feel intimidated by.

It was American decor editor Karen Fisher of *Cosmopolitan* who declared, "Home decorating is the most personal path to self-expression next to making love." I couldn't agree more. Your home isn't about the "right" rug or designer chair, it's about self-expression, creating your own fantasy, and setting out your identity. When we flick through the pages of shelter magazines we often feel pushed to use our homes as public exhibits of our perfect selves. However, this voyeuristic thrill of glimpsing "perfect" interiors seems to have worn off.

The new cost-conscious individuals are no longer willing to conform. They have simply said *no*! They have adopted a touch of the '70s punk rock attitude and have said *f**k you* to designer conventions! There is no longer right or wrong, bad or good. The new story is about freedom of expression and openness.

When you fill your home with beautiful objects, like Rachelle Isherwood and Jimmy MacDonald, the founders of Tent London, even an unhung light can be a beautiful sculpture. Why can't a chair be a bedside table and a stack of books prop up a bed? The result is filled with a warming emotion most of us can relate to. Display what you love and what brings a smile to your face.

Hopeful. Positive

Parisian stylist Sandrine Place has used party decorations to decorate her bedroom wall. "It's not about bringing in the professional tradesmen but giving it a go yourself and being free to self-express," says Sandrine.

This Tokyo bank designed by architect Emmanuelle Moureaux is brightened up by twelve horizontal layers of rainbow colors protruding out from the façade.

Affirmative.

A pinboard is the perfect surface to create a mood board and add interest in the home. London stylist Rebecca McEvoy prefers a space to feel worn rather than polished, giving a sense of history.

Alexandra Meyn—Brooklyn, New York

Exclusively yours

With design being a gauge of cultural mood, the new fearless approach to living and decorating reflects this period of economic collapse and anxious recovery.

"I feel free, calm, and alive when I spend time in my treehouse. I do not live up there in terms of daily storage and clothing and bathroom. It's a very small space. But I do live up there. Meaning, I find my ability to create, have a sanctuary, a place to share and receive, to listen to old records from the thrift store, to host dinner parties, to place a space heater in the colder months, and to lay down where I can see light and leaves," says Alexandra Meyn.

An unemployed interior design graduate, Alexandra Meyn was determined to be upbeat and decided to create her own treehouse in urban Brooklyn. By building it she thought she could also gain some practical skills. "I built the treehouse to keep my mind occupied while managing the anxieties associated with finishing a major life accomplishment (a master's of interior design) amid a hostile economic environment. I wanted to stay motivated, challenged, and committed to a project that reflected my interests and goals. I finished my MBA in 2007 and was unable to find a job in the New York City region (it was bank meltdown after bank meltdown). Luckily, I had applied to Pratt to continue the project I had initiated during my business studies (contemporary real estate options for age-onset) and had gotten in. During my tenure at Pratt, the market hadn't recovered . . . I was in school again with no "experience," and viable internships were scarce. So I decided to make my own and build something that reflected initiative and personal investment. I was in the same position after graduating from Pratt . . . I submitted application after application, but with no internship history or career experience I was hearing only vacuous silence. And so the treehouse took on new ambition, a scope of completion, and a developed goal."

With a budget of $400 she created a 17-foot-/5-meter-tall treehouse cobbled together from recycled materials including wood, tin, and discarded windows she found in reclamation yards.

Amateur design has been surfacing since 2008, rebelling against the theory of polished design. Harmony and balance are passé. Excess is encouraged. Fabrics are mismatched. Paint is smeared haphazardly over walls and ceilings. Our optimistic designers are creative types who fill their rooms with artful clutter—taxidermy, flea market paintings, peeling wallpaper. Personal expression matters more than constructed refinement.

"Decorating is a completely personal expression (much like fashion). If I am lucky enough to have a flourishing career based on my taste and skill, I would advise my clients as I do myself: rules are to be understood, then judiciously broken. Things should have meaning in your space; too many or too few or too "adjective of choice" dilute one's sense of purpose in a space . . . and space, at its best, conveys spiritual and emotional levity to a person's soul," explains Alexandra.

"Decoration came mostly as stream of consciousness within the hems of inexperience and the many factors that can muddle the overall effect inherent in many first projects. However, both the ripped wallpaper and the collages have meaning. The wallpaper (a remnant of Elysian Fields produced by Flavor Paper) is of bats, bones, Venus flytraps, and thorny roses . . . alluding to the dark side of the forest that alerts our inner child and whose name is the same of a major road in New Orleans (where my family is from). I have stacks of magazines and find collage the easiest way to access my subconscious. While there are many things I would like to have done, or wish I had done differently regarding the end decorative result, I appreciate that the finished space is flush with details. The amount of decorative detail has the potential to close in the space rather than open it, but because all of the elements are meaningful to me, and because it is a treehouse, the end result feels very comfortable to me and expressive of what I hoped to gain out of having a treehouse."

**OWNERS: BIANCA RIGGIO + RYAN HANRAHAN
LOCATION: PAGE THIRTY THREE, SYDNEY**

Optimistic design is about daring to be different, about breaking the mold of mainstream design. It is about the individual and it is about the individual making their own statement as to how they decorate. It's time to say to those who are dictating to us that "this is me and this is who I am." It is people like our optimistic homeowners who remind us that while we don't all live in the same decor palace, the meaning of home can be similar. Love your home and the space you live in. It was such a joy spending the day with Bianca and Ryan from design firm Page Thirty Three in their Sydney home and studio. Their space mirrored them as individuals—creative, warm, friendly, filled with humor and love.

Bianca and Ryan decided on their current space through a "change of priorities." To them it was a kind of lifestyle audit with decisions made on the basis of what would be part of their new utopia. If things didn't fit, they didn't stay. As designers they decided to map out their life on a blackboard wall. Starting at the center of the map was utopia. They questioned what they needed to do to be fulfilled. They mapped out how they wanted to live, and their home is a projection of this vision.

When they first moved into their warehouse it was originally a rundown workshop for spray-painting cars and they had to put their heart, soul, and serious hard work into creating a friendly and creative space. Their house is nondescript and anonymous from the street but the inside of the house feels completely private, giving them the freedom to express themselves.

It's time to say to those who are dictating to us that "this is me and this is who I am."

Optimistic Design:
Bianca Riggio + Ryan Hanrahan

_ Pushing aside the gloom and doom

_ Daring to be different and breaking the rules of mainstream design

_ Displaying an attitude of self-empowerment, nurturing an upbeat approach to life

_ Homegrown inventiveness

_ Creating a personal story on every surface in the home

_ Lack of money is no barrier

Starting with a blank canvas, after spending weeks cleaning up the space, they began with the survival basics— a kitchen for food, a safe place to sleep, and a place to wash. Once these were established, they discovered that simple rituals enhanced their life—Bianca always has a good body scrub each morning and both Ryan and Bianca practice yoga and Vedic meditation to start their day, to help them keep that spark of optimism for the day ahead.

The house is filled with plants, as they feel that this connects them to nature and to the outside world, making them aware that we are part of an ecosystem. The indoor garden is on wheels so they can move it around the warehouse, following the sun, keeping in touch with the natural rhythms of the day.

They have used reclaimed and recycled materials, reflecting the interior space as a collaboration of design, art, humor, irony, functionality, and the street. The key for their design inspiration is passion. They have also focused on what they love and keep a clear sense of their style and identity with the aim of creating a space that is welcoming and that contains mementos of experiences that they have shared, such as bathing on a tropical beach or trekking through the jungle or shopping in a favorite city. This leads to another important factor— sustainability in reusing products and being able to pass down what they have to their grandchildren.

Our interiors are an insight into our brains
of design, art, humor, irony, functionality,

t is a collaboration nd the street.

175

PARIS **Be bold with your light fixtures and plugs and let them become features rather than blending into the wall or ceiling.** SYDNEY **A knitted green medicine ball to exercise on suddenly makes hardcore workouts seem like they could be enjoyable. There is no longer a need to try to hide these unsightly objects with this new update by design firm Page Thirty Three.**

INTERNATIONAL TREND
rethink: brights

ACCENT BOLD COLOR

LONDON **Look up! What better way to bring the outdoors inside than to paint your ceiling sky blue. Ceilings often get overlooked but painting them a bold color can give a room the ultimate wow factor. A painted ceiling is a great trick to help make a large room feel cozy.**

MELBOURNE It's a cliché but cushions are one of the easiest ways to add color, humor, and energy into any space. Bonnie and Neil have a great eye in the graphic textiles they design. Mix and match patterns, colors, graphics, and size. Don't limit their use to inside. They are a perfect addition to an outside room.

TOKYO Bold colors contained into areas of a room including doors and windows can be a much stronger choice visually and aesthetically over one feature wall. In a small space it shouts out "look at me" without cracking an eardrum.

MELBOURNE What better way to ground a large white room and fill it with positive energy than by adding a vivacious pink floor. Adding a hue of blue can assure a non-frilly room. A midnight-blue dining table and chairs combined with luscious green curtains make what could have been a stuffy traditional space a modern room with a hint of rebellion.

"Any intelligent fool can make things bigger, more complex, and more violent. It takes a touch of genius—and a lot of courage—to move in the opposite direction."

Albert Einstein, theoretical physicist

rethink
downsizing

The recent mortgage and financial crisis, the troubled economy, and rising costs of water and power have all contributed to the growing trend of downsizing. People are reassessing their lifestyles and the spaces that they live in and how much it is costing.

With an awareness of the increasing population and diminishing resources, the rising cost of housing, and the costs of constantly moving house, people are starting to make use of what they have.

Houses are now being bought as places to be lived in and renovated with the thought of the house being a family home to suit the needs of family as opposed to a saleable investment property, a phase that was popular during the first part of this century. The footprint of our homes is designed smaller to fit our lifestyle.

Living alone is becoming the new norm. Going solo is one of the extraordinary social changes we are seeing. It is becoming more common than the nuclear family, multigenerational family, and having a roommate. In Sweden 47 percent of all households are single-person dwellings.

AVERAGE SIZE OF NEW HOMES ACROSS THE GLOBE			
AUSTRALIA	704/214.6	SPAIN	317/96.6
UNITED STATES	661/201.5	JAPAN	311/94.9
NEW ZEALAND	644/196.2	IRELAND	288/87.7
DENMARK	449/137.0	SWEDEN	272/83.0
GREECE	415/126.4	ITALY	267/81.5
FRANCE	369/112.5	UNITED KINGDOM	249/76.0
GERMANY	358/109.2	*Measured in square feet/meters.	

I came to realize the impact of downsizing when my very close friends in the United Kingdom were living in a one-bedroom apartment.

Within two years, their family unit grew from a couple to a family of four. Not being able to afford to move into a larger home, they had to adjust the space to work for their growing family. To avoid the whole family sleeping in one open space they came up with an ingenious idea of building two pods in the bedroom to give babies and parents some privacy.

Throughout the developed world there are different approaches and cultural expectations of housing and the size of living spaces. It is common in Tokyo to say that a man needs only a place 6 feet/1.8 meters long to lay himself down and take a rest. Designer Natasja Molenaar based in the Netherlands has mounted shelves on the wall for her house cat to use as steps to play and exercise on.

Multigenerational living

Due to the severe economic downturn in the last couple of decades, the multigenerational household is making a comeback in the developed world. In 1940, they made up 24.7 percent of households in the United States, then dropped as low as 12.1 percent in 1980. A study in 2009 by the Pew Research Center, a nonpartisan think tank based in the United States, discovered households made up of related family members had grown to 16.7 percent.

Children are staying home longer, boomerang kids return to the family home, and more families are opting for shared accommodation. Of Australians aged 25 to 29 who live in their parental home, more than half of these have moved out and returned again. Consequently we have seen in this decade the emergence of multigenerational households with the parents housing their adult children (sometimes with their own young children in tow), along with aging parents. This multigenerational household is simply a return to what was once considered the norm.

In Australia nearly one in four people aged 20 to 34 continue to live in the parental home. It's not just those people in their twenties who are staying home. In Australia, 8 percent of Australians aged 30 to 34 are still living at home with their parents.

This "Great Recession" is forcing architects, developers, designers, and homeowners to change their current thinking and examine how multigenerational families interact within a small space and how to extend spaces in existing structures.

A whole family living together is becoming less of a choice and more of a necessity. The option to live in a big house to accommodate all family members is becoming less and less of a possibility.

With apartment living becoming more popular the reality is more people are living in smaller homes. The key is to be focused and selective when decorating the space by not overfurnishing or accessorizing. There are many advantages to living in a compact home. They are more economical to run and you can choose more luxurious materials and high-end details.

**KEY REASONS FOR
MULTIGENERATIONAL LIVING:**

—————————————

**YOUNG PEOPLE CAN'T AFFORD TO BUY
THEIR OWN HOME**

**YOUNG PEOPLE STRUGGLE WITH
RECORD COST OF RENTING**

**SAVING MONEY TO BE PUT TOWARD
A DEPOSIT ON A PROPERTY**

**CRIPPLING COST OF CHILDCARE—A
PROBLEM THAT CAN BE SOLVED WITH
FREE HELP FROM FAMILY MEMBERS**

**NURSING HOMES FOR GRANDPARENTS
HAVE BECOME TOO EXPENSIVE**

These shifts to smaller spaces can have an emotional effect on family dynamics, sometimes causing feelings of resentment and failure in the developed world that is used to accessing more personal space.

Embracing many generations under one roof isn't uncommon to many ethnic groups. In many cultures elderly parents are honored members of the household and adult children are encouraged to stay home and save before buying their own home.

In many Japanese homes it is common to find two separate living areas, one for the parents and one for the younger generation. After marriage the young couple often lives in the same house as their parents.

The NextGen home has had to be rapidly reevaluated using innovative ideas to make a space work for parents and their children's families living under one roof. The new downsized home tackles the shortage of bedrooms, bathrooms, storage, communal, and study areas. Privacy and space are now considered luxuries and creating them is the biggest challenge architects and designers face.

I want families to be aware that they are not alone when they find themselves in a small home. You certainly haven't failed your children if you can't provide each child with a bedroom. With good design and rethinking the layout of the space you live in, it is possible to give your family a fantastic quality of life. Constraints of space often result in innovation.

Privacy and space are now considered luxuries and creating them is the biggest challenge architects and designers face. Savvy space manipulation has been applied by reconsidering things such as the usual width of hallways and depths of cupboards, along with the size and multifunctionality of furniture.

The option to live in a big house to accommodate all family members is becoming less of a possibility.

INTERNATIONAL TREND
rethink: shelving

LONDON Traditional bookshelves are bulky and take up valuable floor space. Recessed bookshelves are a great option to save on space. Photographer Emma Lee has cleverly blended her bookshelf by painting it the same soothing color as her dining area. Her small collection pops out and has become an art installation.

PARIS Don't hide all your books away in cupboards. Keep out the ones you love or want to read in close reach to your sofa. This living room by architect Joseph Dirand is super luxe with the built-in shelves in sophisticated black. They are the perfect backdrop for books and artwork.

PARIS No longer do you need to have newspapers and books stacked on the floor in the most private room in the house. Stylist Sandrine Place has made the most of her tiny bathroom by stacking playful and colorful wooden blocks, making the ideal bookcase built into the wall.

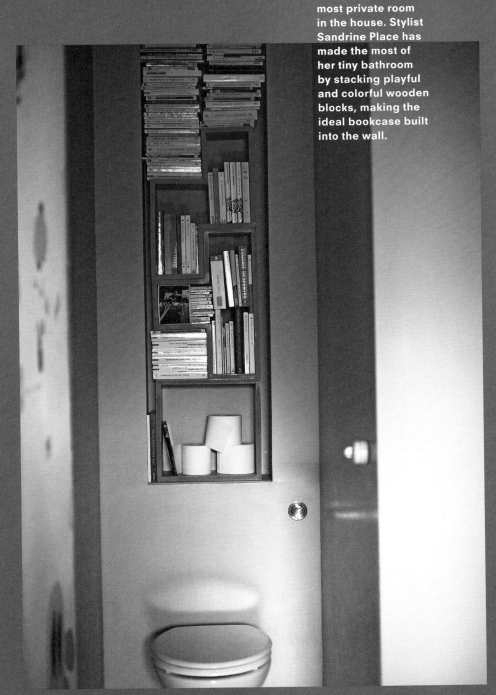

As I write I'm surrounded by boxes and no storage. I have just downsized apartments. Adjusting has been hard: my partner and I love to collect and curate our finds around the home. Tripping over, stepping around, and disguising our much-loved objects that have no home in our new flat is driving me crazy. I keep looking for clever storage solutions but I rent, which limits my options. It's time to consider letting go of the clutter!

With an ever-increasing urban sprawl we need to build small. Living in expensive cities such as Sydney and Tokyo, more people opt to live in apartments that are more affordable. For quality of life people realize commuting long distances to and from work cuts down on valuable personal time.

French designer Paul Coudamy has created this red gloss sliding wall unit combining a bed, desk, wardrobe, and storage in an apartment in Paris. With a floor space of only 248 square feet/23 square meters, the design of the Red Nest has a bookshelf that slides along the wall to reveal and conceal the sleeping, working, and dressing areas. A trapdoor has been used instead of a traditional staircase to help keep the small floor space clear.

The
wet
room

<u>SYDNEY</u> Large Jacuzzi-style baths that ravenously consume water now look dated. To save space, bathrooms are increasingly styled as wet rooms (opposite) where the shower unit dissolves into the fabric

<u>MORIYAMA</u> The bathroom is becoming more of a health room. Using the outdoors for inspiration creates a cleansing environment (below) by including a look-alike natural brook with plants and stones contrasting with your stark white bathroom. Wet rooms are easier to clean since you don't have to worry about

of the room. Choose products carefully. Wet rooms need to look open and sleek, so install a minimal-design tap and shower treated in the same color as your walls. To help make a small space feel bigger include a large window or glass door you can easily open to the outdoors.

shower screens, trays, or tracks. They're also the perfect solution for young children, the elderly, or people wheelchair-bound, as the floor is flat with no lips, hobs, or trays to get over.

Anthony Gill, Sarah McSpadden, and daughter Marigold Gill—Sydney, Australia

Living small with
big thinking

Redesigning a small space for a family calls for innovation and discipline.

The variety of motivations is what makes this downsizing movement so interesting. When visiting small-space homeowners, what was striking was not deluxe fit-outs but how spacious they felt. The key to space faking is being precise, bordering on obsessive attention to detail. No opportunity is overlooked. Every conceivable nook and cranny is used for storage. Every millimeter is used to create more room. No compromise is made on style or comfort. Inspiration for design layouts and fit-outs often came from yacht and caravan interiors. Anthony and Sarah have tackled this scarcity of space in designing their innovative one-bedroom apartment.

Owner and architect Anthony Gill tells his story: "Small living requires mastery over possessions. With the emphasis on economy of space, every inch of space is being used more efficiently in our apartment. Floor-to-ceiling storage is used to hold or conceal accessories, books, blankets, clothes, kitchen accessories, and paperwork. Our extremely small space has a pull-out bed fitted into the storage.

"The redesigning of our small apartment involved transforming an existing 409-square-foot/38-square-meter, one-bedroom apartment in an iconic Australian Harry Seidler building in Potts Point."

"The key to living in
a small space is
you have to be
really disciplined.
Every item we
have has its own place.
In the mornings,
we make sure to slide
the bed back into
place, wash and
put away our dishes
in the kitchen."

The existing joinery (not original) was demolished, leaving only the masonry walls to the bathroom, which remains untouched. A new joinery element was inserted to reconfigure the space, addressing the issues of privacy, storage, and a lack of living space inherent in an apartment of this size.

"Sarah and I are inspired by Japanese architecture that tackles small-space living. The Japanese are masters in successfully being able to make use of and live comfortably in small urban homes. To make our home feel warm and inviting, not cold and stark, we made the deliberate decision not to hide all of our belongings. We filled the new shelving in the living area with loved books and magazines. I am obsessive in how I display the books. I like to order in blocks of color or size to help keep some uniformity to the space. In the kitchen we have open shelves to have easy access to ingredients when cooking. The overall color palette is neutral but by adding a vibrant red Persian rug on the floor and a dusty-pink curtain, a little life is added to the space.

"We selected key pieces of furniture that would give us comfort and work well in our home. We created three living spaces in the main room. Our bed slides away during the day, becoming a play area

for our daughter. We opted for a low sofa to lounge on and a small round table to eat and work from. All the available space was used to its full potential, taking into account our needs and wishes.

"We create illusions to help make the space feel larger than it really is. The best way we have done this is by placing shelving and storage floor-to-ceiling. Our low ceiling loses perspective because the large unit takes over. Having an oversized Noguchi light over the dining table helps direct your eyes out to the view which helps blur the boundaries and make the space feel bigger.

"The key to living in a small space is you have to be really disciplined. Every item we have has its own place. In the mornings, we make sure to slide the bed back into place, wash and put away our dishes in the kitchen.

"We have to respect each other in the tiny environment. Sometimes it can get a bit too much but all we have to do is go for a walk outside and let the other person have some time at home alone."

"I'm obsessive in how I display books. I like to order in blocks of color and size to help keep some uniformity to the space. To open up the kitchen we kept the shelves book-free so we could look in and out and still socialize with the rest of the family while preparing meals."

Instead of using the word "downsizing," the latest catchword is "rightsizing" or "smart living," which describes how many view their choice to change to smaller housing. Economics are certainly a factor contributing to the move toward smaller housing but so, too, are environmental concerns, the realities of inner-city space limits, and personal philosophy. Personal philosophy may be a belief in the benefits of living a less materialistic life compared to the day of the "McMansion." In Tokyo, with the ever-growing demand for housing in the high-density city, families are becoming inventive in how to make the most of their space. Kouji and Keiko Yakuno and their four children live in a little space (their apartment is 769 square feet/71.5 square meters), cleverly illustrating how a family can have a positive experience in a tiny environment they call home.

For most people living in such a tiny space with such a large family would be unthinkable or near impossible in terms of creating a space providing privacy for parents and an environment where children can play, do homework, and be imaginative. The original apartment had walls dividing the living area and bedroom. The architects, miha-design, were given the brief to design a living environment that gave the family a good quality of life, reconsidered the space, and removed all the walls of the original apartment. Two boxes replaced the walls, creating different areas for activities in the room.

Inside the blue "box," there is a bed for the couple and the youngest child. Under the bed, there is a storage space where they can put their things they don't use every day. To make this space feel more open, peepholes have

In Tokyo, with the ever-growing demand for housing in the high-density city, families are becoming inventive in how to make the most of their space while retaining a positive environment.

Downsizing: Kouji + Keiko Yakuno

_ Making use of what they have and making the home suit the needs of the family

_ Designed different areas of the home to have multifunctional spaces

_ Tackled the shortage of bedrooms with an inventive solution

_ Savvy space manipulation has been applied, including hallway width, depths of cupboards, and architectural features

One bedroom per child in the home is not a reality for most families in the world today. It will be more likely in mega-cities that a family will have only one- or two-bedroom apartments.

been cut into the walls, bringing in light. Every bit of space is used, leaving room for the family to walk around the room boxes with ease. The walls of the boxes are used for storage and a kitchen. On top of the box is an area designed as the children's multipurpose space for them to play, read, or draw on the built-in desks. The wooden box also includes beds, desks, and benches for the older three children. This is their private space.

With the top of the box being like a cubby house, the architects have added extra fun and excitement by including a set of small stairs from the living room made from small shelves fixed to the wall to climb to get to the top of the box. When Kouji and Keiko want to check on the children they have to crouch to go up, but for the

children the height is perfect, allowing them to go up into their adult-free area. The lighting has been placed around the apartment strategically so that the children can turn on a light that doesn't "leak" around the whole apartment.

One bedroom for every child in the home is not a reality for most families in the world today. It will be more likely in mega-cities that a family will have only one or two bedrooms. This is why it is so important in rethinking clever and creative solutions to accommodate the whole family and still have quality of life. I believe we will see designers incorporating Tokyo hotel-like capsules in homes where family members can have privacy and quietness when they sleep but have room to live, eat, and socialize in the rest of the home.

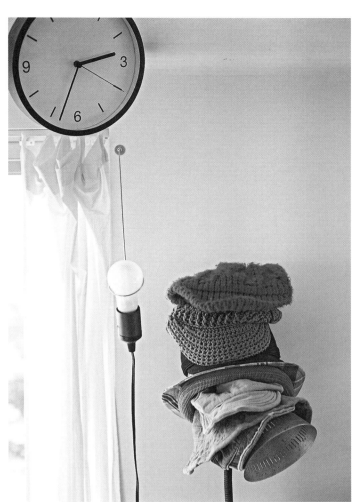

"Understanding
the person or people
living in a home
is a far greater
need in design than
focusing purely
on the aesthetics.
The home is
designed around
emotional needs."

Amanda Talbot

rethink
holistic living

Using the human spirit as a starting point for architecture, design, and interiors is the mantra for this movement. Those successfully creating holistic homes put the human being in the center of the design process for the home.

"People used to want a particular look. Now, they want a home tailored to their lives."

Ilse Crawford, designer

There is a strong focus in domestic design on creating a kind of antidote to the fast-paced and hyperconnected modern world we live in, a world that is filled with phones, computers, and a constant barrage of social media. People are looking for retreats and calming spaces in the home, other than the bedroom or bathroom, where they can completely disconnect and tune out.

In this technological world where it is so hard to switch off, more of us are longing for moments to disconnect and find time for contemplation. American architect David Jameson designed a suspended meditation chamber in this home. This room acts as the spiritual heart of the home where the owners can reflect about life. The internal energy of the meditation chamber is encapsulated within an open glowing frame.

Design that actively facilitates a sense of privacy and respite is becoming a valued commodity. For an American home, "Matryoshka" in Maryland, architect David Jameson created a suspended meditation chamber at the center of the building with the purpose of representing the "physical and spiritual center of the home."

Holistic living isn't new. The biggest change is a growing number of people realizing they want a home that not only fits in with their lives, but is also an environment they can be happy in. It also needs to be a space that is calming and will bring the individual close to the family or group of people they are living with. They want a home that satisfies their needs, that empowers them.

History
Another element of holistic living is the emphasis being placed on a building's surroundings along with the social and cultural history. The homeowners I met believed their buildings have a life and soul. Their job is to animate the feel and mood of the space.

The feel of the street, the neighborhood, and the people that live within it play a big part in connecting the inside space with the outside. Some homeowners pinpoint what they love about their neighborhood and their neighbors, along with natural surroundings, and include elements in their building.

Rituals
It's important to capture rituals, rhythms, and routines played out in the home. Copycats who try to imitate houses found in magazines miss the point. Understanding the content and rituals that work within a home is what gives the design substance and longevity. One of the most prominent rituals in homes across the globe is the making of tea and coffee. Every house I visited had a different procedure and formula in how they made their sacred hot drinks.

We are realizing we want our homes to fit our lifestyles and to be happy in them. A home filled with plenty of natural daylight helps keep a holistic-designed home a calming environment. To bring each family member closer to each other, an open-plan kitchen and living area make it easier for the household to socialize while cooking and catching up on emails and schoolwork.

"The home should be the treasure chest of living."

Le Corbusier, architect, designer, urbanist, and writer

For some a stove-top whistle kettle that was full of old-school charm while in other households a commercial-style barista machine would take pride of place in the kitchen. People are ditching the tea bags and selecting loose-leaf teas and storing them in beautifully crafted containers. Families congregate around the television and dining table at regular times of the day. Domestic duties around the house, from making meals, washing dishes and clothes, to housecleaning, are scheduled at certain times of the day or week. It is with these domestic rituals that more and more people are designing their home, their furniture, and their household items to accommodate these daily activities to the concept in their personal space.

Health and well-being
Individuals who choose to create a holistic home are exploring how to improve well-being and daily health inside the home. Individuals are placing increased emphasis on health and wellness and the need to find time alone.

The fundamental rule is your space should make you feel happy. If we look at cities and how they are often built, they are based on efficiency, pride, and profits, not for human happiness.

For those who want to have a home that brings people together and feel good, it is key to learn from studies from sick patients in hospitals. Mounting scientific proof has shown that well-designed environments can reduce anxiety, lower blood pressure, and lessen pain. It has been proven that patients with severe depression that are assigned a sunny room tend to stay for shorter periods of time. There is now evidence that good design in hospitals can improve a patient's recovery rate. On the other hand, research has shown bad design can produce negative effects, including delirium, elevated depression, and a greater need for pain-relief drugs.

Rituals provide us with a sense of security, stability, and connection. Something we need at great times of change. One of the simplest and oldest forms of ritual is the ceremony of tea making. Making a cup of tea is a chance to have some me time. Depending on the type of tea, it needs to be brewed in a particular teapot, and the water needs to be a certain temperature and allowed to infuse for the right period of time.

HOLISTIC PIONEERS SAY:

I NEED TO UNDERSTAND
THE PERSON WHO LIVES IN
THE SPACE

WHAT IS THE REALITY OF THOSE
WHO LIVE INSIDE THE HOME?

WHAT DO THEY DO?

WHAT MATTERS TO THEM
AND THEIR RELATIONSHIPS
WITH EACH OTHER?

HAARLEM A chic bamboo swinging chair is the perfect reading spot to tuck yourself away in a private nook in the house. Complete the look with a sumptuous and tactile lamb's wool throw and scatter cushion. Make sure you remember to have a side table high enough so you have easy access to your cup of coffee.

PARIS The sound of a whistling kettle boiling on a stove top is filled with old-school charm compared to a flick-of-the-switch electric one. Staring at it waiting for it to boil will of course take longer, but is that such a bad thing? Use this time to stop and contemplate your life and family.

ANTWERP Bathing is one of life's greatest pleasures. The bathroom is your chance to create an environment that can titillate the senses and provide you small luxuries in life. In so many ancient cultures a bathing ritual is the opportunity to cleanse your body, on the inside and out of negative energies and prepare you physically, mentally, and spiritually.

INTERNATIONAL TREND
rethink: rituals

Depression, illness, being over-worked, stress, and unhappiness have become an epidemic due to financial uncertainties. Since 2008, the number of reported stress-related disorders has quadrupled. Statistics from the UK National Health Service Information Center show anxiety disorders and panic attacks rose from 3,754 in 2006 to 17,470 in 2010. It's all too often that the stresses of the day find their way into the very place where we are meant to be the most relaxed—the home. With the rise of technology addiction, our need to check emails, Facebook, and Twitter feeds on smartphones, combined with daily work and life stress, insomnia is on the rise, contributing to major health problems.

This is why so many designers, architects, and nonprofit organizations have become passionate about the importance of good design and how it can dramatically change and improve the mood, health, and well-being of individuals and communities.

A place for self-expression

Inside our homes is where we want to tell our story. It is within the shelter of our homes where we are free to express ourselves and display our collections. From glass cloches housing our bowerbird possessions to tapestries sewn by loved ones displayed on our walls, it is indoors we display our dearly loved objects. It used to be brand names that meant status; now I think that finding that hidden gem is more special. It's no longer about how much you spend, and ultimately that's due to what happened to all of us in the economic downturn.

Designers are exploring how to make individuals find an emotional response to an object or space. The choice of substainable materials, textures, colors, lighting, and a connection to nature are the key ingredients to trigger mood and memories that improve our well-being for daily health inside the home.

In today's busy world it's easy to lose sight of the things that matter: family, friends, your home, you. Modern design is about realigning your priorities to help keep you focused on the important things in life.

Curiosity cabinets and wall installations are the traditional modes of displaying personal treasures, but increasingly compact modes of urban living mean that contemporary collections are often spread out.

The result is a shift away from static, formal collections to something more akin to ongoing interior conversations, relaying a greater sense of artistic aspiration throughout the space.

Collecting isn't hoarding. It's about surrounding yourself with objects that make you feel happy.

The thing is, although many of us don't have the disposable income we once had, it doesn't mean we don't want nice things around us. We have to work harder now in how we present those nice things, but the outcome is becoming much more rewarding.

Merchandising tricks in retail are resurfacing as a major trend in the home. What may look odd in single format can be transformed by multiple groupings. In Melbourne, Bonnie and Neil have created a wall of gaudy tapestries that establish a unique mood. Glass cloches filled with bowerbird finds are displayed in Martin and Patricia Willem's home in Antwerp.

THE NEW FORTRESS

I'm known to be a professional "snoop" and I love walking past other people's homes during dusk to view, from the street, how others live their lives. Families sitting around the table eating or watching television, someone working at their desk, or a couple having an argument. I adore seeing how people decorate their homes, especially in homes I know I could never afford. It has always fascinated me but it looks like this pastime may be coming to an end. Ever heard the saying "don't judge a book by its cover"? Now the same can be said about the home. In cities all over the world with homes surrounded by noise and traffic, more people are wanting their homes to be closed off from the outside as much as possible. The exterior designs are becoming antisocial, even unfriendly from the street—almost a "no trespassing" kind of sign. Internally the design is a stark contrast with the spaces being open and light, conveying the feeling of warmth and friendliness.

Welcome home. I hope that's how you will always feel here. From the moment
you walk under the rosy Albertine archway and enter the front door (it's green
this week, but you know that's likely to change), that's what I want you to
feel. Welcome.

Our home is forever changing, but that has become our "the same." You may come
home to find the furniture rearranged, or a different color, or gone for the
night (sorry, Annebelle, but your bed really was the perfect prop for a shoot).
What is constant, though, is how we sit at that same dinner table every night,
bump into each other in the kitchen every morning, and jostle for position in
front of the bathroom mirror every morning. Yes, it's tight, but we wouldn't
see each other as much if we had more rooms, would we?

I love how you girls have approached the decoration of your own rooms. Annebelle—
your room is so you—elegant, young, and color-coded to the extreme. Everything
matches. Alex, what can I say? I sigh as I trip over the elaborate dollhouse setups
and wince as I look at the walls covered in posters, but really, you are just
doing what I do—twelve-year-old-style.

My happiest memories of us here are nearly all centered around the lounge/
dining/office/piano room. That poor room really takes a beating. It's where we
all hang out and do our thing. It's where we eat, watch TV, listen to music,
make music, dance, cuddle the animals, and I work. It's where we talk. It
really is our "living room."

I know when I am home, my shoulders relax and my eyes delight at the color. I
really believe in the power of color. It uplifts, it soothes, it satisfies. I hope
our home has the same effect on you guys. I hope it is your refuge and somewhere
you can happily bring your friends and know that they, too, are always welcome.

I hope that our approach to life as a family—our philosophies and our beliefs—
are ingrained in our home. Girls, if you can learn anything from our home that
will help you make good life choices, I'll be really happy. This is what I mean:

*If you can't do both, and you have to choose between travel and a new bathroom,
always take the plane ticket. Chipped tiles and a leaky tap won't ever enter your
mind when you are discovering a new place 5,000 miles away (and you're more than
likely to come home and find those quirks quite charming).

*Know that the thickness of the marble on a kitchen bench is no measure of the
happiness inside a home or the mark of a person who lives there.

*Nobody has to love your home but you. Have the confidence to zig when others zag.
Hold on to things that mean something to you (no matter what they look like).

*Collect. Collect whatever you love. By surrounding yourself with the things that
you love, your house will always be your home.

Love, your
wife and mother,
Heather x

Heather Nette King, Jeremy King, daughters Annebelle (15) and Alexandra (13), along with Sugar the ginger cat and Dougal the golden retriever

design for the senses

More and more people are using their senses to influence the design of their homes. With the increase of digitalization in our lives there is a need for the tactile and the textural. When we touch surfaces that are rough or smooth, hard or soft, natural or can be one of the most powerful triggers to remind the brain of a memory. Taking inspiration from the past we are now looking for alternatives to the scented candle to add fragrance in our built environment.

manmade, they give us a connection to nature or soften the hard building features within a house. The basic needs for a human are safety, security, happiness, connection, joy, love, food, water, and health. Our home is the one space we can have and contain our human needs. Smell

The French King Louis XIV (1638–1715) would commission a new scent every day, ordering his perfumer to scent pieces of court furniture. Today's technology makes it possible to repeat the Sun King's extravagance and embed soft furnishings with scent during textile production.

Our bedrooms may be getting smaller but our beds are getting bigger. The king-size bed, being nearly 7 feet/2 meters wide, is killing off the traditional double bed that was once considered the only bed a couple would need. The trend in having a king-size bed is growing, as it allows people to re-create the luxury of sleeping in a large hotel bed. Parents are opting for them to allow their small children to climb in at nighttime without disturbing everyone else's sleep.

Beds are the ultimate multifunctional piece of furniture. We eat, entertain, and reproduce in them. You might have been conceived in one and will probably die in one. We spend roughly 3,000 hours a year sleeping in one. It's where you spend most of your time with your partner and where you often bond with your children. Today, a bedroom has become more than just the place we sleep in. These supersize beds have become the focal point and social space of the room. Bedroom design is replicating the feel of a hotel suite with the appropriate bed so that families can use this space as a communal space, watching television or spreading out work papers and a laptop.

INTERNATIONAL TREND
rethink: emotive

<u>NEW YORK</u> **A dog is meant to be man's best friend. If you already live with a dog or cat, you know how easily the furry friend becomes a member of the family. I have even heard that owning a pet can make you happier, healthier, live longer, and weigh less than people without pets.**

AMSTERDAM
Handwriting is an endangered species. This is why when we do see a note, poem, or quote inscribed by hand it gives the message so much more meaning. It brings the human spirit back and can make it feel like it has more meaning and individualism.

SYDNEY Smell is one of the most potent triggers to transport you to a place or feeling you love. Using natural scents to calm, invigorate, balance, or focus throughout the day is a beautiful way to bring wellness into your routine. Test and try different oils and burn them in a beautiful essential oil burner like this one by Page Thirty Three.

Find the light

Clever design means this hidden home is flooded with light, providing a source of energy that drives the growth and activity of this Japanese family's home.

"Let's build a happy and bright house," said architects Takeshi and Megumi Hosaka to their client Keigo Nishimoto, his wife, and two children. The two-story home is surrounded by a mix of buildings ranging from ten-story apartments to office buildings. The residence stands on a foundation that sits a story below street level. With the potential of the home being dark, gloomy, and not very private, the architects focused on illuminating the interior space with natural daylight by installing 29 skylights throughout the entire home instead of using traditional windows. Upon entering the building, there is so much light from the sky that it is hard to believe that the site is nested in a dark valley created by the surrounding buildings.

Nishimoto Family—Yokohama, Japan

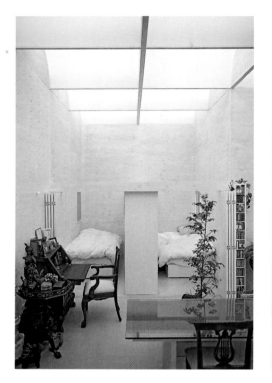

This house was named "Daylight House." "Daylight does not simply indicate direct light from the sun, but refers to the beautiful light throughout the day," says Megumi.

It was key to feel the subtle and dramatic changes of sky and connection to the outdoors inside the home. "When it comes to the ceiling, it is a white acrylic vault board ceiling enabling the projection of the subdued expression of light and sky coming through the glass skylight on the ceiling surface. In addition, the holistic approach to materials in the mortar floor and larch plywood wall combined with strategic lighting; the surfaces blend harmoniously, providing an abstractness, as if the light and expression appear at the upside of the inside space." Takeshi Hosaka used other clever ideas to watch the sky as it changed throughout the day by designing a reflective glass dining table so when the family sat down to eat at different times of the day they could experience nature without the need to look up.

A narrow staircase reaches a slim garden in the front, creating a private entrance. The outside of the building is wrapped in a skin of metal panels and has an unassuming street façade.

There are no views through windows of the domestic space within. However, the inside has been designed with all the family's needs, providing a warm, inviting, and secure place to live in and spend quality time together.

The architects sensitively interpreted the needs of the family and designed the bedrooms and an area for private studies with an open ceiling space. Featuring large folding doors, the spaces can be fully incorporated into the main living space or closed off for privacy. A loft level partially sits on top of the children's bedroom and serves as a neutral platform for multiple functions. With all the needs delivered and keeping to the original promise, the Nishimoto family has a home that offers an environment to be happy in and that filters in plenty of light.

This calming home in a busy city proves we can still have connection to nature without being exposed to neighbors and traffic. Creating peaceful, restful, and private spaces inside while keeping the buzz outside out is the new design challenge we face.

OWNERS: YOSHINOBU + AKIKO KATAOKA
LOCATION: TOKYO, JAPAN

We once wanted our whole home to express our personalities. We wanted to be noticed. We wanted our home to show off the money we spent on it and to show we kept up with the Joneses. How times have changed. More and more people are opting for the outside of the home to be anonymous or nondescript. It is as if we have built a protective shield outside our house; we don't want to let strangers look in on the life inside. Yoshinobu Kataoka's home nestled in a busy Tokyo street doesn't give away how he shares his home with his wife, Akiko, and their two young children, aged four and six.

"We designed the home to have no windows on the front wall of the house so the owners had plenty of privacy. However, from the street a passerby can see some greenery and there is a gap in between the crowded neighboring houses. With the house being located in a shopping district of Tokyo, we made it possible to secure some sense of open and closed at the same time," says architect Yukio Asari from Love Architecture Inc.

The inside is a completely different story. When you walk into this fortress-like home you are greeted with an environment of warmth, friendliness, love, and personality. Yoshinobu and his wife, Akiko, wanted a house that wouldn't fall into decay. They didn't want a minimalist home but wanted it to be full of life. They believe the best way to educate their children is by not hiding their lifestyle. It is filled with loved and used pieces including antique collections, children's artwork stuck to the window, and well-used saucepans hanging above the stove.

Now, more than ever, our homes are the one place where we can be ourselves and escape from the craziness going on outside. It's the place where we can let go and just be.

Holistic Living:
Yoshinobu + Akiko Kataoka

_ The outside of the home is antisocial and closed off while the inside is warm and inviting
_ Plenty of room for self-expression
_ Calming rooms inside to help disconnect and tune out
_ Designed a space to work with the family's rituals, rhythms, and routines
_ Created a home they feel happy in
_ Vistas of nature with plenty of daylight

"This house is open not just in the living, dining, and kitchen but also in Yoshinobu and his wife's atelier. It is an important factor to link each family member within the space of the house," says Yukio.

However, Yoshinobu and Akiko still wanted some privacy in the home. "Everyone is an individual human being or a couple before being a family member. It is important to secure a space where they can spend their time alone or as a couple. Yoshinobu had a clear vision for his bathroom where he wanted to be able to have quiet time and gaze out over his street filled with shoppers when taking a bath and then be able to walk out onto his balcony with a beer afterward," says Yukio.

Behind closed doors, this modern-day home is warm and inviting, designed to encourage social interaction between members of the family. Throwing the house keys on a table and sharing the day's events, sitting and watching television together, gathering around a table talking and eating food lovingly made is important to this family like so many across the globe wanting to feel nurtured and needed.

The vertical green wall outside is visible from every room through the soaring glass walls. The light floods in, making the home light and bright, and the green, living wall prevents an unsightly view of a brick wall. This home may be cold on the outside but there is no question that the inside is beating with a generous heart.

More people are wanting their home to [...]
the outside but keeping the inside open [...]

be closed from
ight, and friendly.

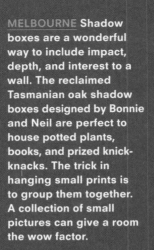

INTERNATIONAL TREND

rethink: wall art

HANG A COLLECTION

MELBOURNE
Sometimes more is more and can be so right. To help break up the repetition in a cluster of artwork, paint your walls. Famous galleries across the world don't stick to stark white to display art but use hues that complement the masterpieces that are hung on them.

HAARLEM Old unwanted empty frames of all sizes and shapes painted the same color as a wall can be the perfect addition to any room. You can find gorgeous ones at yard sales, flea markets, thrift stores, and online. Sand them, paint them, and hang them in a group. **AMSTERDAM** China is best when it is used. It's time to raid your mom's and grandparents' cupboards and pull out old saucers and hang them on the wall to create a pretty display.

TOKYO Give your kids' art a proper display space in the home. Create a zone for the artwork where they can see it and share it with the rest of the family. You never know, you might have the next David Hockney living near you. **PARIS** Don't let the lack of a frame put you off displaying your family snapshots, invites, or cards. A bit of tape or blue tack is a great substitute if it means you can look at your travels and much-loved mementos instead of tucking them in a cupboard.

"I'm constantly connected when home. In the kitchen I look up recipes and Skype colleagues. In bed I order groceries and write. I never switch off. I can't think of a better place to be productive and creative."

Amanda Talbot

rethink working from home

Home offices are fast becoming the rule rather than the exception. Some 10 million Americans already operate a business from home. More importantly, at least 15 percent of workers spend at least one day a week doing work at home.

Around 34 million Americans—about 11 percent of the working population—telecommute on a regular basis. By 2016, that number will have swelled to 63 million—around 21 percent of the working population. This prediction is one that will be mirrored globally as flexible working hours and conditions become acceptable to a wider group of employers. Advances in technology make it easier than ever to work at home without giving over your life—or your house—to your job. You can live like a freelancer with the perks of a corporate executive.

Decide how you prefer to work:
Do you like somewhere to stand and work on the computer?
Do you need privacy to concentrate?
Do you need a meeting table for clients and staff?

BIG IDEAS: AMAZING THINGS HAPPENING

The home office is set up in a professional environment so the homeowner can hold meetings with clients.

With today's technology often a traditional study room is no longer needed as people will work from a bed, dining table, or a sofa in front of the television.

As in the corporate world, desks are set at standing level to help with work flow and saving on space.

SMALL IDEAS: HOW YOU CAN ADAPT THEM

If you invite clients to your home, decorate your office so it reflects your brand and your home.

Install streamlined integrated technology so you can work anywhere you desire around the home.

As the number of homes with access to broadband infrastructure grows, working from home has become more viable. With better wireless Internet connections, the emergence of smartphones and tablets as viable business tools, and cheap productivity applications such as Skype, Dropbox, and OpenOffice, it's much easier to work while on the move.

Companies are realizing that by allowing their staff to work from home it can help save office costs, ease traffic congestion, and enable employees to manage their workloads more effectively. IBM saved $56 million a year after reducing office space by 2 million square feet/1.9 million square meters.

In 2011, UK Business secretary Vince Cable announced plans to change the UK law in 2013 to give every employee the right to request a flexible working pattern. Flexible working has transformed the lives of many, particularly those with parental or caring responsibilities. For small businesses wanting to reduce overheads it's not an uncommon practice to move the office into the employer's home. Dining rooms or front rooms in the home are taking on the look of professional working spaces. A conference desk now replaces the dining table for client meetings or providing a space for staff to work around while private living quarters are commonly found upstairs.

Self-discipline when working at home is important so you work within "work" hours and switch off after hours so that work doesn't spill over into the personal. Having a separate space in the home where you can shut the door after work hours is a simple physical act that helps your brain shift into "home" mode.

Whether you have a whole room or just a corner, your home office needs to inspire you. If you will be regularly having clients over and staff working in your home office, create a room that has a professional vibe mixed with your personal home style. An L-shaped desk is a practical choice for a dual-purpose space, as it can be tucked into a corner.

MELBOURNE A simple yet stylish ceiling-high bookcase provides plenty of storage. Why not make a feature wall out of your shelving? Color blocking is a great way to create visual impact and help keep open shelving feel neat and tidy. Bright accents can help keep up energy levels and motivation to make sure you hit those deadlines.

ANTWERP Hide most of your work behind cupboard doors. But remember when creating a home office to warm it up with some favorite books, mementos, and natural wood. To streamline your design, use hanging shelves attached to a wall unit. You can double the capacity of your shelving by layering books and accessories.

INTERNATIONAL TREND
rethink: home office

<u>LONDON</u> **Keep the creative juices flowing by pinning up tear sheets from magazines, papers, and whatever else inspires you on a wall directly above your desk. Paint your shelving and desk in the same hue as your walls so they can blend in and not overtake a small room. Trestle tables are a great, affordable option that can easily be pulled down if you need to turn the space into a guest room.**

Sandrine Place—Stylist, Paris

Working wireless

Establish new work spaces without dedicating an entire room to a working day.

The downside to working from home is missing the social interaction and the buzz of a work-place. There is an exciting range of work spaces emerging where entrepreneurs, freelancers, and those simply looking for a change of scenery can go to network, collaborate, or seek inspiration. A growing trend in opting for mobile devices is giving people flexibility to move from office to home, a coffee shop, or coworking space.

The reality is that many of us don't have the space to dedicate a room to the home office. Desks are being replaced by the dining table, sofa, or bed. Work spaces operate within open-plan settings for a more flexible layout. Psychological boundaries are becoming an important factor in separating the domestic life from the professional life.

Designers and architects are exploring compact and efficient ways to soundproof, block out distractions, and heighten concentration when working in an open-plan space. Physically separating the at-home work space—whether by using pods or rooms-within-rooms—can help to establish these vital psychological boundaries which, in turn, boost productivity.

Heidi Dokulil—writer, editor, curator, publisher, Sydney

"My home office is my hub, it has all the tools and technologies I need. Technology is key. Being connected is the secret to a happy home office," shares homeowner Heidi Dokulil from the one-bedroom Sydney home she shares with architect husband Richard Peters.

Heidi is one of Australia's leading lights when it comes to the Australian design scene. She is cofounder of Happy Talk and the Australian Design Unit, a member of the Pecha Kucha Night committee in Sydney, and editor of a number of online design publications including *More Space* magazine for the retailer Space Furniture.

"I had more of a traditional studio for the previous six years but technology allows for an elastic way of working. Increasingly I was holding more meetings in cafés than my office and I also wanted a far more flexible place to base myself."

Heidi loves the freedom of being at home and working in a space that she has helped to shape with the things she loves. "I also think that domesticity is nurturing and aids creativity in a work scenario. I particularly love having a kitchen so my clients and I can cook and have lunch together. I think my clients and I have better and more creative meetings here."

Richard and Heidi have designed a quiet room for their home office with filtered natural light, ventilation, and a view to a neighbor's jasmine vine. Files are tucked away in concealed storage and key pieces of art pop color into the space. Underfloor heating keeps feet warm in winter.

"I'll transfer to
the laptop and work
in other rooms
if I want a change.
I like moving
around, especially
if I'm writing."

"My survival tip for working from home:
I hide the vacuum cleaner, laundry, and other things
that remind me of housework. I like to
have music playing to match my mood, a candle
burning, flowers from the garden on my desk,
and a fresh cup of my favorite tea."

Dorthe Mathiesen—set designer, Copenhagen

With space being so precious, finding room for a home office can be next to impossible. An unassuming nook could be the answer for an inspiring working space. Dorthe Mathiesen has used her creative skills and created a desk that can also function as a "mini" lounging and storage area. The storage stairs to the "mini" lounge can easily be moved aside to get to the six big plastic drawers, filled with books and magazines hidden inside the back of them. "I love to sit up by the window and 'load my batteries' or meditate, hang out, research online, have a nap or a good conversation with my fellow roomies," says Dorthe.

Dorthe has broken down how she prefers to work and created an area where she hasn't made any sacrifices. She has the option to sit or stand when she wants to concentrate on her precision drawings or sit back and relax while she surfs online. "I must have a big table when I'm working so I have enough space for magazines and books to spread out. Lighting is key and it's important to have a good task light over the table. I also like to be surrounded with inspiring and personal stuff, with good energy and karma."

Brian Jones—Intel business development manager, Oberselters, Germany

With four generations living in one house, privacy is everything to keep a family happy. Six people live in this home: Brian Jones, his wife, two children, and his wife's mother and grandmother.

Brian has been the business development manager for Intel since 2006 and he is responsible for the German channel: marketing and technical projects. When he briefed architects Reinhardt Jung, Brian requested the entrance to his office have separate access and as much privacy as possible to help him concentrate in a quiet and calm place. "We decided not to situate Brian's office on the main floors. We rather extended the levels further down and decided to use the old backyard of the house on the basement level to create a separate unit as a one-room office with a Zen garden in front to bring daylight into it," says architect Alexander Jung.

To help Brian focus and be productive in his working environment, raw materials including cool concrete have been used to help enhance the silent quality of the outdoor space, which is framed by a gabion wall. The office has a light rail that allows Brian to plug in technical instruments wherever he wants.

"What I love about this German home office is the two little niches designed in the space. One is a room for the copy machine, server, and materials, and the other—13 feet/4 meters high—is a place to relax and hang out to do some reading next to the Zen garden. This is the perfect idea for those of us who don't have the space for a separate room to work from. Setting up space like this is the perfect area to work from and have a little privacy from the household rush."

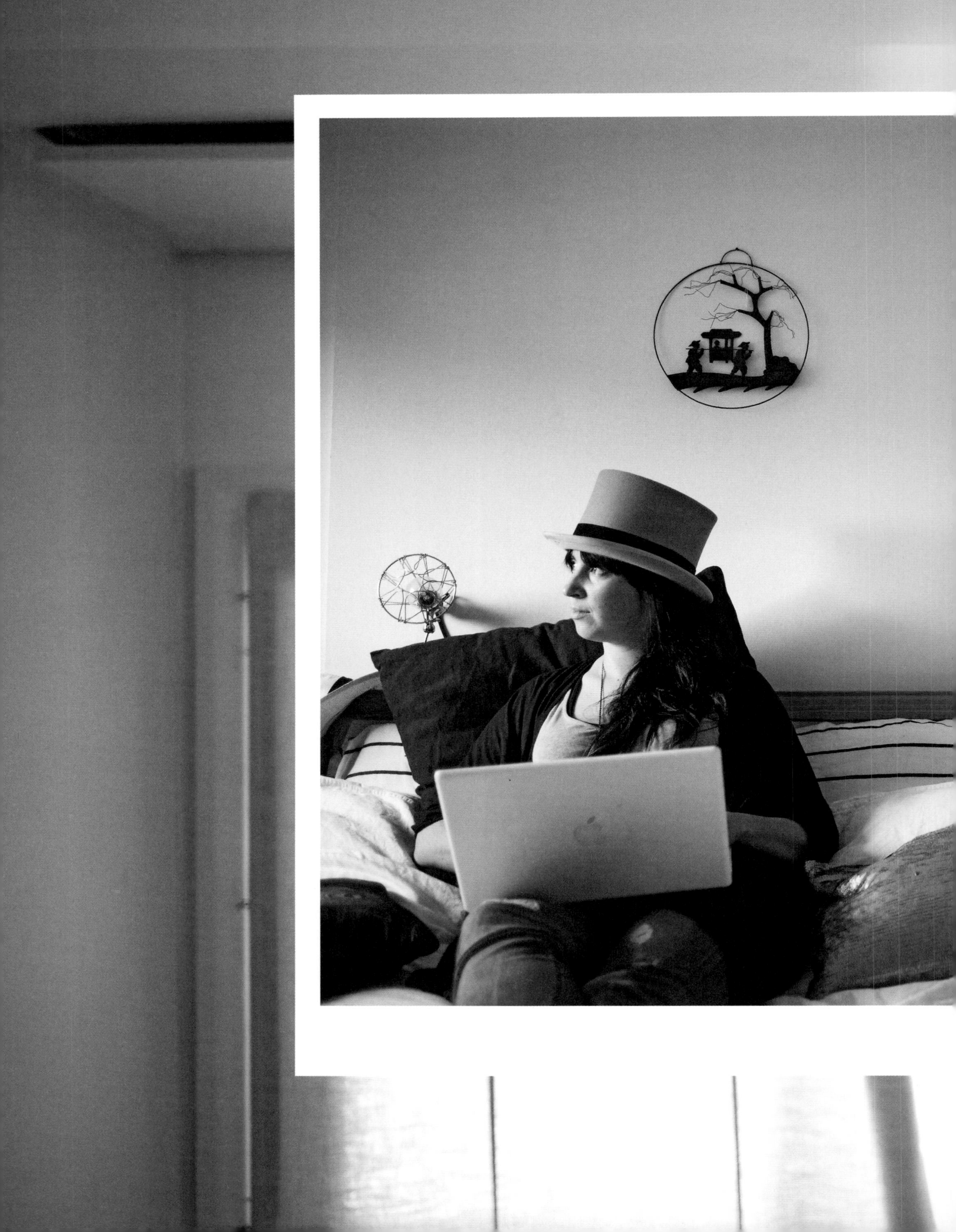

Rebecca McEvoy—stylist, London

Rebecca McEvoy was head stylist for iconic design store Habitat and style editor for British *ELLE Decoration*. Now she is a freelance interior stylist working with some of the world's greatest brands. When Rebecca isn't in her studio working she opts for her bed in her little one-bedroom flat as her home office. "I work from my phone and my laptop. My phone is so handy to keep on top of things when I'm on the move—I'm just really bad at dropping or losing them. I think it is more of a luxury than a necessity to have a dedicated space to work from. All I need is a digital radio, big cushions, clamp-on bedside lights that double up as task lights, and lots of cups of tea." And what is the best benefit for Rebecca working from her bed? "I can work in my pj's and no one knows!"

"Develop a specifically
tailored approach that
is customized to your
work–life philosophy
so that you can work
cohesively. Create both a
successful operational work
environment and
also meet individual
family needs."

Michael and Tessa Bautovich—designers, Sydney

Many of the greatest brands started out from the home. Google was created from a garage, IKEA from a toolshed, Jo Malone from a dining room table. Sydney couple Michael and Tessa started a children's design company, Lowercase, from their ground-floor Paddington home in Sydney. "We started our business at the same time as a new generation of design-conscious and environmentally aware parents were emerging. We have quickly developed a cult following that has inspired us to expand product lines to meet more new demands of the modern family environment," shares Tessa.

The terrace-studio conversion welcomed a customized space that expresses the couples' personality and is synonymous with their brand: creative, intuitive, and functional. "This has allowed us to be relentless in our pursuit of good design and escape any of the opposing creative constraints and doctrines associated with a traditional office space, so we are simultaneously living and designing a creative lifestyle 'outside the (office) square.'"

The kitchen is no longer just the heart of the home but the heart of Michael and Tessa's business. In their open-plan kitchen they have set up laptops on a white, modern sleek table where they keep an eye on their little toddler, Xavier, who plays on the floor beside them. Their smartphones sit next to the keyboards to answer customer, media, or manufacturing inquiries. "As night falls we unwind by changing the music to classical and replacing the myriad computers, laptops, and iPads with tea-light candles," tells Tessa.

"We are spending nearly every waking minute online. Our home used to be the place we switched off but not anymore." The King family is one example of how a family works and lives at home.

"Annebelle is obsessed with her Tumblr page. Alex is a massive Skyper and loves playing on kids' fashion sites such as Stardoll. They'll be doing homework on one screen, with other screens minimized with Facebook or something similar. They'll also be texting their friends and listening to music on their iPhones. I wish I had their multitasking skills!" shares mom Heather.

Smartphones, computers, televisions, game consoles, and iPads are changing how the family behaves inside the home. Dictionaries and encyclopedias are no longer found on bookshelves. It's not just our kids who are busy online at home. Most working mothers and fathers I know will usually get dinner ready, do some house chores, eat with the kids, make sure their children are doing homework, and then hop online either by phone or laptop and catch up on emails, write up reports, socialize on Facebook or Twitter, and create a blog post.

"It's a familiar sight to see all of us on some kind of wireless device at the same time in the same room. Diminishing levels of family interaction used to worry me, but now we have a few 'technology-free' times each day, and technology rules: there is no technology allowed at the dinner table; the girls must leave phones and computers outside their bedrooms when they go to bed. I don't think the levels of technology have hindered our conversations."

"Try to have your home office in a separate room. Sometimes I think it would be heaven to be able to close a door on the noise. But it's a luxury we don't have, so you just learn to work with what you've got."

Working from Home: King family

_ Access to broadband has made working from home more viable

_ Created different work environments for each member of the family

_ Dining table, beds, and sofa are all being used to work on

_ Dedicated plenty of storage and non-distracting folders to store paperwork

PARIS A stylist said to me the other day "vintage is dead and overused." I say NEVER. A good eye will always see the potential to bring something back to life. Look out for old lampshades and bases you can spruce up to take pride of place.

rethink: mood

WORK / LIGHT BALANCE

AMSTERDAM Diffused lighting is one of the best ways to light your home office. It will illuminate the whole room without creating hard edges. Make sure your light output covers your entire working area. Create a feature of your desk by hanging two stylish pendant light drums above it. It will definitely wow your visiting clients.

NEW YORK Natural light is the best way to light your study during the day. Remember it is better for the eyes if you have general background lighting on when using a desk lamp. Pick a bold colorful desk light to add a cheerful accent to your work space.

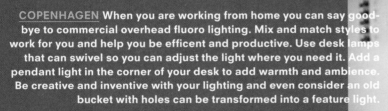

COPENHAGEN When you are working from home you can say good-bye to commercial overhead fluoro lighting. Mix and match styles to work for you and help you be efficent and productive. Use desk lamps that can swivel so you can adjust the light where you need it. Add a pendant light in the corner of your desk to add warmth and ambience. Be creative and inventive with your lighting and even consider an old bucket with holes can be transformed into a feature light.

"Urban nomad:
A new generation
of worker/travelers,
they transplant
themselves to new
cities across the
globe following
the next big career
opportunity."

Urban Dictionary

rethink
mobile living

Across the developed world, mobile living is on the rise and at the forefront of design. Floating homes, prefabricated homes, temporary homes of all kinds address the need for new and innovative designs for housing.

Nomads have been around since early civilization. Pastoralists would wander from place to place looking for new grazing lands for their herds. Their wandering lifestyle meant that they lived in temporary shelters and their travel was dictated by the seasons and cycles of nature. Minimal possessions meant they could pack up and move when it was time. With the rapid change of technology and the "nomadic" existence of global workers in developed countries in the 21st century, we are likely to become mobile, no longer staying in one city or town or even country.

Houseboat living is no longer the domain of retirees. Young and ambitious water residents are exploring courageous design for their homes normally found on the land. This 21st-century approach to designing a home on water is making nomadic ideals a possibility for a modern family who is not prepared to sacrifice quality of life while moored or on the move.

We have become urban nomads moving to cycles of opportunities in an international job market.

Urban nomadism is also developing as part of an ongoing shift from rural to city living: 60 percent of the global population will live in cities or be commuting between them by 2030, according to United Nations research.

Today flexibility and mobility have become key concepts of the working world. As a result, the "traditional" idea of possessing a house along with accumulating household goods is shifting. Urban nomads have overcome temptations of consuming so they can move and change. They have considered what they essentially need to be able to live on the move and how their furniture and small number of possessions should be designed to accommodate their nomadic existence.

In 2004, an escalation of house prices sparked the craze for living on water. Today, with the burden of first-time buyers needing to find hefty deposits before they can apply for a loan, living on water is the perfect solution to owning a home in a city center that would usually be priced above a young professional's budget. A state-of-the-art canal boat in the UK costs around half the price of an average inner-city apartment. The possibility of buying a houseboat for roughly $67,000/£40,000 and being free from a loan and mortgage and having disposable income is an attractive prospect instead of being a slave to pay off debt. The image of houseboat living is no longer the domain of retirees. In 2004 British Waterways registered that 15,000 people were living aboard canal boats in the United Kingdom.

These days the current problem is, with a new demand in houseboats, residential mooring is like gold dust. From Paris, Copenhagen, and London to Australia, there are not enough sites deemed to be suitable to live on.

Living in a floating house, houseboat, or barge is not a new idea; it has become a revamped idea. What is new and different about living at a floating address is the up-to-the-minute technologies, materials, and design choices that architects and designers are creating for homes on the water. Sublime finishes and 21st-century technology are being integrated into an efficient use of space, turning the clunky boats into luxuriously appointed floating apartments.

The interiors of this houseboat, by Piet Boon, moored in the Dutch waterways are designed to the level of his award-winning houses. The designer kitchen and seating area blend seamlessly into the enclosed outdoor patio. The simple ambience has been achieved with minimal styling and key pieces of furniture.

Today it's not always about planting your roots. With more people traveling constantly between mega-cities for work following their next career opportunity, it is not surprising people are looking for short-term accommodation options, including fully furnished apartments, mooring, or parking a mobile home.

With cities across the globe becoming so overcrowded we are seeing architects and designers looking for alternative housing solutions to cramped apartment living that suit transit workers who are always on the move.

Home is a transit lounge.

Home is a transit lounge

When it is time for heading off, urban nomads simply pack a couple of suitcases, shut the doors of a shipping container, or pull up anchor. Being able to move house spontaneously gives this group of nomadic dwellers a sense of security, of having a home base, and of being able to transport important and loved possessions easily along with the freedom to move when they need to and not being tied down by a huge mortgage.

Shipping containers

The shipping container is affordable and adaptable. Across the globe designers and architects are adapting containers and transforming them into award-winning homes. At $835 per container, building a house becomes more affordable and within the reach of many people wanting to live in the city.

What I love about containers is you can gradually extend. Shipping containers are made to standard measurements that can be combined into larger structures, which is as simple as stacking containers. This simplifies design, planning, and transport. They can be stacked up to twelve high when empty. Prefabricated containers can be easily transported by ship, truck, or rail.

Collaborative consumption

One fast-growing trend in this movement is collaborative consumption. More and more people in urban areas are sharing ownership of possessions with others in the community. For example, instead of buying tools there is an option to rent them from a community tool shed. Car sharing programs are growing rapidly in urban areas. It is amazing that you can access a local car with the swipe of a card and drive off for a little less than the cost of a taxi.

Belgium-based architects SCULP(IT) have proven our future way of living should be inside the box. Their home and HQ for their office in Antwerp's former red-light district is made from four stacked shipping containers. With the plot of land only 7.9 feet/2.4 meters wide their only option was to build up. The four-story home sandwiched tightly between buildings represents four different working and living spaces.

SCULP(IT)

Huikstraat 47
Antwerpen

www.sculp.it

vernieuwend

interieur

SILVIA MERTENS, ARCH.
PIETER PEERLINGS, ARCH.
TEL/FAX 03 289 07 24
WWW.SCULP.IT

"Convenience," "time saving," and "cost" are the three magic words for the current times we live in.

The average American moves 11.7 times in a lifetime, according to the United States Census Bureau 2009 report. This works out to about one in six Americans moving each year.

It's not just Americans whose homes are becoming more transitory. According to the 2006 Australian Census, 40 percent of the population moved in the five years between 2001 and 2006, while 16 percent of people moved in the one year between 2005 and 2006.

With so many of us on the move it is not at all surprising that we are trying to find inventive solutions to create ease and savings in often-frequent relocating.

The reality for the urban nomad is their geographic movement usually happens with short notice. Ease of moving and getting to their new address quickly is essential for this lifestyle. Shipping containers are an easy option for transportation and German inventor Daniel Straub has designed an amphibian caravan, "Sealander," that goes from land to sea with ease and without modification.

Floating homes

Living on water gives hope to urban nomads for flexible living and battles overcrowding in high-density cities.

Water is the next frontier for architects looking to provide viable solutions to making the most of areas for urbanization. Creating communities on water has the potential to alleviate a range of problems associated with high-density urban living, such as overcrowding. By harnessing the properties of water, architects, urban planners, and environmental experts may be able to create more environmentally friendly solutions to climate change.

With sea levels rising as a result of global warming, the low-lying Netherlands is fighting back by building communities on water. Instead of trying to hold back the water, the Dutch are trying to live on it. Architectural firm Waterstudio is the world leader in building villages on water. The houses are linked together by walkways and can be detached from the surrounding neighborhood and individually moved by tugboats.

Watervillas, Waterstudio, Amsterdam

Sustainability is much more feasible on water because of its natural qualities. Harnessing solar power and the natural sea breeze makes it easier to control the climate within communities and individual buildings.

It's an idea that could significantly shape the future development of large international cities, 90 percent of which are fringed by large bodies of water, including the supercities of London, Tokyo, and New York.

An Australian company called Solar Sailor has developed hybrid boats that could be the future of marine travel. The technology is similar to what is used for hybrid cars. Sails covered in solar panels can be hoisted up to harness the power of the sun and wind. Electricity is generated by the solar panels, then stored in a battery that drives the boat engine. Using the elements of nature creatively reduces the human reliance on fossil fuels that are in limited supply.

"Water is the next frontier for architects looking to provide viable solutions to making the most of areas for urbanization."

PLUG-IN CITY
LOCATION: TOKYO + BEYOND

Portable housing is a radical and revolutionary way to live, but where can our land nomads park their homes? Architects are exploring how we can move our home place to place, plugging the building into an urban vertical trailer park. Since 1965, Archigram envisioned the Plug-in City that separates land tenure from housing form. The Polikatoikea concept designed by Filipe Magalhaes and Ana Luisa Soares for the Origami Competition used Le Corbusier's Domino house, Kisho Kurokawa's Nakagin Capsule Tower, and IKEA's prefabricated home for inspiration to provide cheaper, more flexible housing. The designers envision platforms that act as yards where you park your tiny prefabricated home.

On a larger scale, Brazilian architect Felipe Campolina explored portable units that can be plugged into a steel-framed skyscraper. Again the idea is to own your own unit but rent the parking space and connection to services. The units are transported and delivered to site, similar to a pop-up camper that extends when connected up to a campground.

Architects have conceptualized plug-in cities since the '60s with empty frameworks holding dwellings in the form of cells or standardized components that could be slotted in. The question is, are we really ready for this extreme style of living? Or will it always be science fiction and a futurist's fancy?

Portable housing is a radical and revolutionary future way to live, but where can our land nomads park their homes? Architects are exploring how we can move our home to a new town and plug into a vertical trailer park.

Mobile Living: Plug-In City
_ Able to move at a moment's notice
_ Helps with accommodation relief for a growing shift from rural to city living
_ Provides flexibility and mobility
_ Encourages collaborative consumption schemes including car sharing and clothes swaps

"A hundred years ago people certainly had a connection to nature. They were aware of the seasons and aware of what they were doing to the land and animals around them."

Sir David Attenborough, naturalist

rethink
the future
home

So what does the home of the future look like?

Rethink is a glimpse into the homes of people and an insight into the new ideas that will shape how designers, architects, and people of all stripes will approach living in a sustainable way.

The biggest challenge to be tackled right now and well into the future is protecting the planet, and this can be done by consciously focusing on living with a very small carbon footprint.

Earlier chapters focused on the emerging trends that are propelling design and living revolutions in our urban spaces. From guerrilla gardening and nurturing spaces to mobile living and down-sizing, these are innovative ways that people are coming up with to tackle the environmental, living, and working conditions that we face.

Fossil fuels make up approximately 95 percent of the world's energy use. As our world consumes more and more of these to fuel our everyday lives, these resources are running out. What we have are finite resources. Once they are gone, they are gone. Forward estimations predict that these resources will last for only a relatively short time.

WORLD ENERGY CONSUMPTION WILL INCREASE BY 36 PERCENT BY 2035.

WITH OUR FOSSIL FUELS RUNNING OUT, RENEWABLE ENERGY SOURCES—WIND, SOLAR, GEOTHERMAL, HYDRAULIC, TIDAL, WAVE, AND BIO-GAS—WILL HAVE TO PLAY A CENTRAL ROLE IN MOVING THE WORLD ONTO A MORE SECURE, RELIABLE, AND SUSTAINABLE ENERGY PATH.

Modern design is all about limiting the use of nonrenewable resources and increasing the use of renewable energy resources, along with a strong nod to sustainable living practices.

In the future home, standard buildings will include low carbon emissions, reliance on renewable energy, and the use of clever design, incorporating elements like solar panels. Materials will be either recyclable or will not end up in the landfill at the end of their life cycle. The future home is also about individuality and the push away from the mass-produced or current fads in design.

Individuals across the globe are proving that you can live sustainably in an urban environment by changing your lifestyle habits. Incorporting solar power, energy-saving appliances, water collection, waste water processing, vertical gardens, and even chickens will help lead you down the right path. With a new high demand for these products and methods, we are starting to see prices drop down, making them affordable.

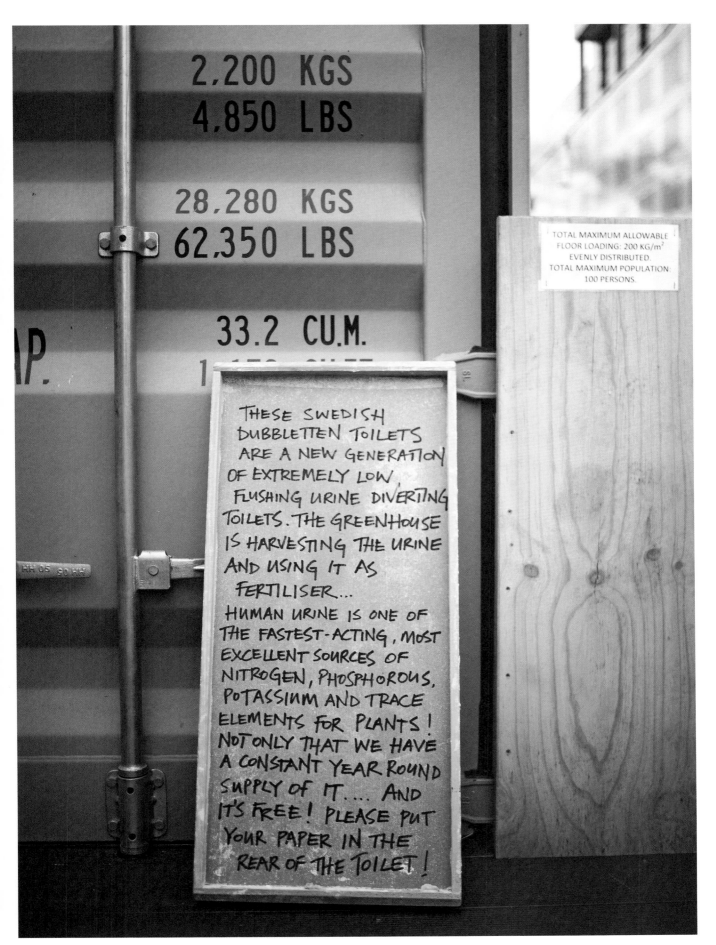

2,200 KGS
4,850 LBS

28,280 KGS
62,350 LBS

33.2 CU.M.

AP.

TOTAL MAXIMUM ALLOWABLE
FLOOR LOADING: 200 KG/m²
EVENLY DISTRIBUTED.
TOTAL MAXIMUM POPULATION:
100 PERSONS.

THESE SWEDISH DUBBLETTEN TOILETS ARE A NEW GENERATION OF EXTREMELY LOW FLUSHING URINE DIVERTING TOILETS. THE GREENHOUSE IS HARVESTING THE URINE AND USING IT AS FERTILISER...
HUMAN URINE IS ONE OF THE FASTEST-ACTING, MOST EXCELLENT SOURCES OF NITROGEN, PHOSPHOROUS, POTASSIUM AND TRACE ELEMENTS FOR PLANTS! NOT ONLY THAT WE HAVE A CONSTANT YEAR ROUND SUPPLY OF IT.... AND IT'S FREE! PLEASE PUT YOUR PAPER IN THE REAR OF THE TOILET!

Passive solar buildings are being created, eradicating the need for fossil fuels to heat or cool a house.

Villages, cities, and towns are being created to be sustainable.

SMALL IDEAS: HOW YOU CAN ADAPT THEM

Invest in low-energy and low-water consumption appliances.

When building, extending, or renovating consider how architecturally you can include wind turbines, solar panels, and insulation.

Focus on insulating to keep heat in and make use of heat gains from daylight and stoves.

Rethink is a small window into what the future of the home will look like and how the individual will live in the new cities within this personalized sanctuary.

A general awareness of the limited resources that fuel our cars and homes is becoming more widespread as the cost of conventional energy is rising. The increased cost of food, the miles it travels, and where it has been grown and treated are other factors pushing us toward sustainable food-growing practices and our own self-sufficiency, seen in the increase of backyard or balcony vegetable gardens. There is the worrying realization that the resources that we have taken for granted are now seen to be finite and there is a strong possibility that these resources will run out. This brings the question of survival much closer to home. People are concerned about their environment and how they will survive in a world that is rapidly changing.

Those wanting to make a small difference are buying less, using less, monitoring usage, changing lightbulbs, and insulating their homes. Awareness is growing that if you slash energy use in the home, you will save money on gas and electricity and also make a dent on emissions.

Households now have access to appliances that are lower in energy and water consumption. Food, shopping, cooking, washing-up, and laundry choices are helping to reduce the impact of carbon emissions. Modifying behavior by reducing the length of showers, switching off toasters, kettles, microwaves, and other appliances at the power source, recycling and reusing all contribute to living a more sustainable life. Every little bit helps.

Awareness in not showering too long, switching off the lights, turning off appliances at the power source when not using them, or turning down the central heating or air-conditioning. All these acts help us move toward living a more sustainable life and contribute to making people more aware of the footprint they leave on the planet. New homes are beginning to integrate carbon calculators and water monitors.

The One Tonne Life House, built by wooden house experts A-hus to plans drawn up by renowned architect Gert Wingårdh, was built to show it is possible to live in an environmentally friendly modern home. Wingårdh has created an unexpectedly luxurious feeling of space while including solar cells and green electricity. The house's volume is emphasised by its all-white interior, flowing spaces, and double-height 23-foot/7-meter stairwell, on a relatively modest 840-square-foot/78-square-meter footprint.

"Living at the 1.5-tonne level was an extreme experience for us."

Off the grid

There is a growing global community of people who want to do what they can, when they can, to help save the planet and stall the effects of climate change. They are using design to fuel their ideas, providing a blueprint for the world they would like to live in.

Brands, architects, and designers are collaborating closely to prove that it is possible to make green living easy, affordable, accessible, and desirable. In Sweden, in January 2011, a project was launched called "One Tonne Life," to prove a family of four could reduce the amount of carbon dioxide footprint from 7.7 tons/7 metric tonnes per person, per year, to just 1.1 ton/1 metric tonne. This amount corresponds to the level that will be necessary in order to slow the impact of climate change.

Over six months and with the project completed in July 2011, the Lindell family, who were chosen for the project, didn't make it to 1.1 ton/1 metric tonne. In order to reduce their emissions still further, in the final 1.7-ton/1.5-metric-tonne week the family chose to reduce the size of their home by closing off one room and all its amenities. "On our way down to 2.5 tonnes (2.8 tons) we didn't have to make any major compromises in our everyday lifestyles. After that, however, things got tougher. Living at the 1.5-tonne (1.7-ton) level was an extreme experience for us," comments Alicja Lindell.

With the right know-how, the right technology, an awareness of how carbon dioxide is produced, along with consistent behavior focused on minimizing the carbon footprint, it is possible to change carbon behavior without significantly changing one's lifestyle or standard of living. However, human habits and building design do need to change. An example of this change is the WestWyck Eco Village founded by Mike Hill in Melbourne.

WestWyck Eco Village

Many of us read about new developments being created to produce eco villages, towns, and citites. However, in inner-suburban Melbourne, Australia, maverick Mike Hill has created his own eco village called WestWyck. He has created a project that is influential in setting new standards for quality sustainable design and sustainable living.

Sweden's "One Tonne Life" project has proven it is possible to change carbon behavior but the biggest challenge is not the technology but human behavior. To try to reach the 1.1-ton/1-metric-tonne level of carbon dioxide per person can be an extreme change in lifestyle. With mavericks in our communities such as Mike Hill, who designed WestWyck Eco Village—efficient in materials, water, and energy—there is hope.

WestWyck village now occupies the building and grounds of the former Brunswick West Primary School. The school ran out of students in the 1980s and threatened to become yet another example of quality inner-urban infrastructure that had lost its original function and faced the bulldozer. Instead, the WestWyck developers aimed to bring the building to new and vibrant life as an urban demonstration showpiece of sustainable development and good design.

The key sustainability principles that justify WestWyck being termed an "eco village" are "materials efficiency," "energy efficiency," and "water efficiency." The new dwellings are designed to high standards of energy efficiency. The water management regime is pushing new boundaries in reducing reliance on water mains and minimizing the discharge from the site of water via the stormwater and sewerage systems. The construction phase has reused and recycled where possible, making careful decisions about the sourcing of other building products and reducing the amount of material going to landfill. The apartments and townhouses are built as healthy homes with careful application of benign materials and finishes.

An eco village aims to provide an element of community. The first stage of the development will comprise a housing cluster of five new townhouses on the school grounds and seven warehouse-style apartments skillfully designed into the classrooms and corridors of the Victorian-era school building. All dwellings include a private courtyard terraced area. Within the grounds there are shared productive and recreation spaces landscaped largely with local native or productive plants.

WestWyck also aspires to relate to the local community, benefitting the local economy and making use of local infrastructure including the superb public transport options. Local workers and local tradespeople have been engaged and appliances and fittings have frequently been sourced from local suppliers.

Some common design features of the future home will include:

Passive solar building design

In passive solar building design, otherwise known as climatic design, windows, walls, and floors are made to collect, store, and distribute solar energy in the form of heat in the winter and to reject solar heat in the summer. Unlike active solar heating systems, it doesn't involve the use of mechanical and electrical devices. Our future homes are about science and harnessing the natural environment. Designers and architects are focusing on understanding a combination of climatology, thermodynamics (heat transfer), and passive movement of air and water without the use of electricity, fans, pumps, air-conditioning, or heating. Taking advantage of your local climate is the key to designing a passive solar building. Elements to be considered include window placement and double glazing, thermal insulation, thermal mass, and shading. Passive solar design elements are easily incorporated into new buildings and retrofitting existing buildings is becoming standard practice.

Cradle-to-cradle

Cradle-to-cradle design focuses on a product having a full-cycle life and never ending in a landfill. In 2003, architect William McDonogh and German chemist Michael Braungart wrote a manifesto stating, "Today with our growing knowledge of the living earth, design can reflect a new spirit." So instead of living in a system of "takes," "makes," and "wastes" there is a possibility of reinvention for human designs. Within this framework we can create economies that purify air, land, and water that rely on current solar income and generate no toxic waste, that use safe, healthful materials that replenish the earth or can be perpetually recycled, and that yield benefits that enhance all life. We are already seeing intelligent products entering the marketplace made from biological and technical nutrients including a fabric known as "Climatic Lifecycle," which is the first 100 percent biodegradable commercial upholstery. Carpet brand Zeftron is producing commercial, durable carpets that have an ongoing lifecycle. At the end of the cycle of the carpet, the manufacturer takes back the carpet and reuses the materials in another high-quality product. Raw material to raw material is the true essence of cradle-to-cradle.

The home of the future is not as sci-fi as we imagine. Instead of whizbang gadgetry and the bells and whistles reminiscent of *The Jetsons*, the home of the future is all about sustainability, energy-efficient design, an expression of the individual, and a hotbed of creativity and inspiration.

Smart and sustainable technology as a design feature

Modern buildings have been incorporating smart and sustainable technology on the inside for a while now. Now—thanks to advances in materials, renewable energy systems, and even biology—sustainable technology is no longer an afterthought or a tack-on, and homes are more likely to receive dramatic makeovers on the outside. Architect Chad Oppenheim from Oppenheim Architecture + Design has designed COR, a green residential and commercial tower in Miami. This building of the future has energy-efficient elements that play an integral part of the design. The building extracts power by utilizing the latest developments in wind turbines, photovoltaic panels, and solar hot water generation. Other ideas are designs making use of both sky and the ground to generate and conserve power. Solar panels are being used as architectural features and green gardens are cared for on the roof of buildings to help contain thermal control.

RETHINK: HOW WE
ARE REINVENTING
THE WAY WE LIVE

LIVING TRENDS ARE
CHANGING RADICALLY IN
RESPONSE TO THE HUGE
GLOBAL CHANGES
AFFECTING OUR LIVES

LEARNING TO BUILD A BETTER
WORLD FROM THE GROUND
UP. GOING BACK TO WHAT
NURTURES, PROTECTS, AND
MAKES US FEEL SAFE

FINDING A SENSE OF CALM
AND CONTROL IN A WORLD
FILLED WITH EVENTS THAT
ARE UNCONTROLLABLE

LEARNING TO ADAPT
TO A RAPIDLY EVOLVING
ENVIRONMENT

REVOLUTION:
DISCOVERING NEW WAYS
OF REMODELING OUR
WAY OF LIVING AND BEING

THANK YOU

Thank you to the team at Murdoch Books: Chris Rennie for first seeing the potential of RETHINK, the beautiful Tracy Lines who believed in, drove, fought for and inspired me, and held my hand to craft a book. Sophia Oravecz and Jody Lee for making sense of my words.

The amazing and patient design team from Ikon.

To my London crew, Nikki Docker, Rowland Scott Smith, Alfie, Catherine Higgs, Alastair Scott, Jacky Parker, and Despina Curtis, who provided me with their wonderful hospitality and sofa to rest my head.

To my Sydney crew, who have supported my return back to Australia and make me feel so welcomed.

To all my followers on Twitter and blog SnOOp who helped me find so many of the individuals and families who are featured in RETHINK.

Gerome Heath, Geri Chipova, Sophia Heath, Michael, Sarah, Oliver and Imogen Heath, Phinnaeus O'Connor, Josephine and Charlie Cobb, Wendy Talbot, and Bernard and Julie Hunn for their support.

Mikkel Vang, who survived earthquakes, snowstorms, and an author nose-planting headfirst on a road in Antwerp to photograph this book. You are a superstar!

To everyone who is featured in this book. You all have been my inspiration and give me hope that our world in the future will be okay.

EMERGING TRENDS
Edward do Bono, **Think! Before It's Too Late,** Vermilion, UK, 2009.

Marco Buti, **Quarterly report on the euro area, European Commission, Directorate-General for Economic and Financial Affairs,** vol. 10 no. 4 (2011).

www.harvardsquarelibrary.org/unitarians/cannon_walter.html

www.notable-quotes.com/g/global_warming_quotes.html

Nick Squires, **"European crisis: protests and violence on the streets in Italy and Greece,"** The Telegraph, UK, 17 November 2011.

LIVING WITH NATURE
Sir David Attenborough, **BBC Frozen Planet**, 7 December 2011.

Ilse Crawford, **Home Is Where the Heart Is**, Rizzoli, New York, 2005.

Ferris Jabr, **"Can a Stroll in the Park Replace the Psychiatrist's Couch?"** Scienceline, 12 August 2010.

Thoraya Ahmed Obaid, **State of world population 2007: Unleashing the Potential of Urban Growth**, United Nations Population Fund, 2007.

Anjali Rao, **Tadao Ando Talks Asia Interview, CNN World**, April 11, 2007.

Frank Lloyd Wright, **"In the cause of Architecture,"** essay for Architectural Record, March 1908.

www.futurefoundation.net

BACK TO BASICS
Amanda Talbot, **interview with Stephen Bayley, British Elle Decoration**, October 2008.

CREATE AND CONTROL
William Glasser, **Choice Theory: A New Psychology of Personal Freedom**, HarperPerennial, New York, 1998.

Margarita M. Posada, **"Ergonomics for the aging population: Implementing methods to maintain quality of life,"** Human Factors and Ergonomics Society, National Ergonomics Month, Fordham University, 2003.

www.searchquotes.com

SELF-SUFFICIENT LIVING
The Economist, **"The Adoption of Genetically Modified Crops, Growth Areas,"** 23 February 2011.

European Parliament, **Parliament Calls for Urgent Measures to Halve Food Wastage in the EU,** Plenary Session, 19 January 2012.

Food 2050, Feeding 9 Billion, **"Urban Farming for Food Security?"** August 17, 2010. http://food2050.eu

Clive van Heerden, **Philips Design press release**, 9 December 2009.

How to Feed the World in 2050 Report, Food and Agriculture Organization of the United Nations, 2009. www.fao.org/fileadmin/templates/wsfs/docs/expert_paper/How_to_Feed_the_World_in_2050.pdf

Mary Clare Jalonick, **"How Much Do Americans Waste on Food?"** Associated Press, 4 June 2013.

Rachel Nugent and Axel Drescher, **"Urban and Peri-Urban Agriculture (UPA) on the policy agenda: Virtual conference and information market,"** Sustainable Development Department, Food and Agriculture Organisation of the United Nations, October 2000.

Resource Centres on Urban Agriculture and Food Security, **"Why is Urban Agriculture important?"** 2005. www.ruaf.org

Kevin Rudd, **"The Rumble of Hungry Bellies Grows Louder,"** The Daily Telegraph, 11 October 2011.

United Nations, **"World Population Will Increase by 2.5 Billion by 2050,"** United Nations Press Release, POP/952, 13 March 2007.

United Nations Environment Programme, **"State of the Environment and Policy Retrospective: 1972–2002,"** 2002.

United Nations Population Fund, **"Linking Population, Poverty, and Development,"** 2007.

Worldometers, real time world statistics. **www.worldometers.info**

Worldwatch Institute, **State of the World 2007.**

WRAP, **Material Change for a**

Better Environment, Food Waste Report, The Food We Waste, 2008.

OPTIMISTIC DESIGN
www.brainyquote.com

Douglas Coupland, **"A Dictionary of the Near Future,"** New York Times, 12 September 2010.

DOWNSIZING
www.alberteinsteinsite.com/quotes

Australian Bureau of Statistics, **4102.0—Australian Social Trends, Home and Away: The Living Arrangements of Young People,** June 2009.

Bina Brown, "**Boomers Go Bust Over Kids,"** Sydney Morning Herald, 11 September 2011.

Alejandro Lazo, **"Putting Extended Families Under 1 Roof,"** Chicago Tribune, 22 November 2011.

Paul Taylor, Jeffrey Passel, Richard Fry, Richard Morin, Wendy Wang, Gabriel Velsco, Daniel Dockterman, **"A Social and Demographic Trends Report, The Return of The Multi Generational Family Household,"** Pew Research Center, 18 March 2010.

HOLISTIC LIVING
David H. Barlow, V. Mark Durand, **Abnormal Psychology: An Integrative Approach**, Wadsworth Publishing, 6e, 2011.

www.brainyquote.com

Laura Donnelly, **"Anxiety Disorders Have Soared Since Credit Crunch,"** The Telegraph, 1 January 2012.

Robert N. Golden et al, **"The efficacy of light therapy in the treatment of mood disorders: A review and meta-analysis of the evidence,"** American Journal of Psychiatry, 2005, 162:656–62.

Health.India.com, **"Anxiety disorder cases on the rise since 2008 global recession,"** 1 January 2012.

Joint Commission Resources, **Care Delivery and the Environment of Care**, Illinois, 2003.

R. Ulrich, **"Effects of health facility interior design on wellness,"** College of Architecture, Texas A&M University, 1991, 1992.

R. Ulrich, **"Effects of interior design on wellness: Theory and recent scientific research,"** Journal of Health Care Interior Design, 1991, 3: 97–109.

WORKING FROM HOME
InnoVisions Canada, Canadian Telework Association, **Saving Office Space & Innovative Office Strategies**. www.ivc.ca

Michele Pelino, **Demand Insights: Enterprise Mobility 2009**, 28 July 2009. www.forrester.com

Graham Snowdown, **"Work from Home Day: Let's Do It Again,"** The Guardian, 20 May 2011.

MOBILE LIVING
Australian Bureau of Statistics, **3412.0—Migration, Australia, Population Mobility 2007–08.**

www.boatsville.com

www.ebay.com

Jimmy Lee Shreeve, **"Canal Boat Living: Rise of the Eco River Gipsy,"** The Telegraph, 26 November 2008.

United States Census, **Geographical Mobility / Migration, 2010 to 2011.**

WaterStudio, **Vision, Koen Olthuis,** www.waterstudio.nl

THE FUTURE HOME
Sir David Attenborough, **BBC Frozen Planet**, 7 December 2011.

International Energy Agency, **World energy consumption—World Energy outlook 2010 Factsheet: What does the global energy outlook to 2035 look like**, 2010.

William McDonogh & Michael Braugart, **Cradle to Cradle, Remaking the Way We Make Things**, North Point Press, 2002.

www.onetonnelife.com

WorldWatch Institute, **Making Better Energy Choices**, Global Energy Use Trends. www.worldwatch.org

First published in the United States of America in 2015 by Chronicle Books LLC.

First published in Australia in 2012 by Murdoch, an imprint of Allen & Unwin.

Text copyright © 2012 by Amanda Talbot. Photography copyright © 2012 by Mikkel Vang (unless stated otherwise).

Library of Congress Cataloging-in-Publication Data is available.

ISBN: 978-1-4521-3919-7

Manufactured in China

Designed by Kate Dennis, This Is Ikon

Additional photography: Bere architects, page 29 (bottom); David Jameson, pages 207, 209; Emmanuelle Moureaux, page 135 (bottom); Filipe Magalhaes and Ana Luisa Soares, page 286; HK Honey, pages 109 (top right; left, 2nd-last row from bottom), 122; i29 Interior Architects, page 140 (center); Michelle Kathleen Anderson Photography, page 115 (right); One Tonne Life House project by A-hus, Vattenfall, and the Volvo Car Corporation, pages 296, 297; Page Thirty Three, page 103 (center, photographer Bianca Riggio); Piet Boon, pages 274–5 (photographer Richard Powers, styling Karin Meyn); Reinhardt Jung, page 259; Sealander, page 281 (top); Suppose Design Office, pages 29 (top), 51, 138, 139, 141 (right), 193 (photographer Toshiyuki Yano); UID Architects, page 31 (photographer Hiroshi Ueda); Yasutaka Yoshimura Architects, page 281 (bottom).

10 9 8 7 6 5 4 3 2 1

Chronicle Books LLC
680 Second Street
San Francisco, California 94107
www.chroniclebooks.com